# FROM WORK TO RETIREMENT

Marion E. Haynes

**CRISP PUBLICATIONS, INC.**
Los Altos, California

# From Work
# to Retirement

**Editor:** Beverly Manber
**Designer:** Interface Studios
**Typesetting:** Interface Studios
**Cover Design:** Barbara Ravizza

Copyright © 1993 by Crisp Publications, Inc.
Printed in the United States of America

Crisp Publications, Inc.
Menlo Park, California

Library of Congress Catalog Card Number 91-07078
Marion E. Haynes
From Work to Retirement
ISBN 1-56052-145-7

# Preface

This book will help you make a successful transition into retirement. It will make you aware of alternates that are available to replace the role of work in your life. As you respond to the exercises and complete the questionnaires, you will have a better understanding of your retirement and what is required to have a creative, productive retirement life, which encourages continued intellectual growth. After reading this book, you will know what you can expect as you move from your career into retirement.

You will find very little theory in this book. Instead, you will discover practical, detailed guidance on how to enter the third phase of your work life. Part I gives you a perspective on retirement today. It looks at the very important role work has played in your life. Part II explores the transition experience, first generally and then at work and at home. Part III introduces a wide array of alternatives to work, including:

- Income Producing Activities
- Volunteer Activities
- Leisure Activities
- Hobbies
- Educational Activities
- Athletic Activities

Plans need to be written down. Part IV is a guide for planning and a format recording your retirement plans.

Use this book as a catalyst for self-examination, problem-solving and planning. By completing the exercises you will get maximum return on the time you invest in reading. The exercises are an integral part of the total learning experience. As you study the information, apply it to your own experience and record your conclusions, you will become involved personally in the process. Before you begin, find a pencil and get ready to look personally at your own attitudes and expectations about retirement.

The generation of Americans approaching retirement today is in a unique position. Pension plans, improved working conditions, increased attention to diet and exercise, and the trend to smaller families have produced a generation of healthy, financially secure people. We have tremendous potential to enjoy a retirement not generally available to most workers around the world, nor to prior generations here at home. At the same time, we can make a contribution to society. The message of this book is: *Make the most of it. You have earned it.*

Marion E. Haynes

Springdale, Arkansas

# Contents

PART I

# The Realities of Retirement Today

*Chapter 1* _____

# *Understanding Retirement*

Ideas about retirement are changing. It is no longer a relatively short period of time, when you can walk in the park, doze before a fire, fish or play a few rounds of golf. Today, retirement can span a third or more of your lifetime and offer unlimited opportunities for fulfillment. (See Figure 1-1).

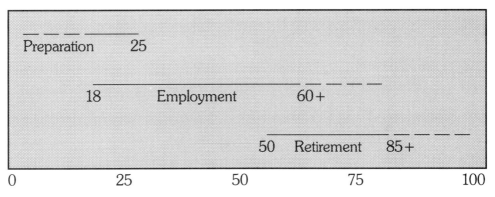

Preparation     25

18     Employment     60+

50     Retirement     85+

0        25        50        75        100

**The Three Phases of Working Life**
**Figure 1-1**

Most people are well acquainted with the first two phases of the life cycle: following a period of preparation appropriate to your chosen career, you become employed. This book addresses the third phase of your life—retirement.

## A NEW CONCEPT OF RETIREMENT

Retirement, as we know it today, is a new concept. Therefore, we have few role models to follow. At the turn of this century, the at-birth life expectancy for American men was 45 years. That did not leave much time for retirement. Men typically worked until they either became disabled or died. On the average, for the few who made it, retirement lasted less than five years. Can you recall your grandfather retiring? What about your father?

### Life Expectancy

Things are different today. The at-birth life expectancy for American men is 74. Those who make it to age 65 can expect to live to 80, while women can expect to reach 83. (See Figure 1-2.)

This is only part of the story. The fastest growing group in our population is 85 years and older. Two hundred and ninety-four people celebrate their 100th birthdays each week. There is a lot of time left for the typical retiree today. In fact, it is not uncommon to be retired for as many years as one was employed.

|  | White Men | Other Men | White Women | Other Women |
| --- | --- | --- | --- | --- |
| At 60 live to | 78.2 | 77.0 | 82.6 | 81.2 |
| At 65 live to | 79.8 | 79.1 | 83.7 | 82.7 |
| At 70 live to | 81.7 | 81.5 | 85.1 | 84.5 |

**Life Expectancy at Specific Ages**
**Figure 1-2**

Today, because of better medical care, improved diet and increased interest in physical fitness, more people are living longer and reaching the ages of 65, 75 and older, in excellent health. The activities and attitudes of a 70 year old today are equivalent to those of a 50 year old a decade or two ago.

## Recent Changes

Following World War II, four major changes altered the way we viewed the retirement years:

- The number of people 65 and older grew from 18 million in 1965 to 30 million in 1990. This age group now comprises 12 percent of the population. It is expected to grow to 21 percent by the year 2030.

- The number of people 65 and older in the workforce declined from 50 percent in 1948 to 16 percent in 1989.

- The financial, physical and mental health of older people improved. A long life became something to look forward to, rather than dread.

- Researchers gained a much better understanding of aging and the lives of older people. This helped to sort out the results of biological aging from the effects of illness or social and environmental problems.

As a result of these trends, many of today's retirees are emerging into truly golden years. They are younger and healthier than their predecessors. Their children are reared, careers completed. They have adequate finances and time to enjoy the fruits of their labor. Through careful planning and management, they are making retirement the best years of their lives.

## Retirement Defined

What is this thing called retirement? Do you envision it as a time of leisure? Perhaps you have observed your colleagues' retirement and have formed some ideas of what it is. In the space below, write your definition of retirement:

**My Definition of Retirement**

_____

_____

_____

Here are some definitions that communicate the different aspects of retirement:

- Retirement is a natural rite of passage, experienced by people as their careers come to a close and they move on to new opportunities.

- Retirement is leaving the organization after qualifying for immediate pension benefits.

- Retirement is the reward for completing one's career.

- Retirement is the *opportunity* to engage in meaningful activities and pursue one's dreams: it is *freedom* from organizational constraints and family responsibilities, and it is *choice* to select the path one will follow into the future.

Compare your definition to these. Do you want to rewrite your definition to incorporate a positive view of the future?

## Making the Transition

A successful transition from work to retirement is not as easy as many people believe. However, with some soul-searching and careful planning, you can make your life after your career a rewarding and satisfying experience. You stand at the threshold of opportunity: how you choose to proceed will determine whether your retirmeent is filled with growth and excitement or stagnation and boredom.

The transition from work to retirement involves moving from one set of comfortable circumstances to another. This process takes a year or two for some people; others may never find their niche beyond work. Like most change, the transition can be unsettling. You can expect some emotional peaks and valleys while you search for your new identity.

### Requirements for a Successful Retirement

A rewarding, satisfying retirement depends upon three basic requirements—your financial, physical and emotional well-being. You need adequate financial reserve and good health, and you must *also* make the necessary emotional adjustments. This will include such things as developing a new personal identity apart from your career, leaving colleagues behind and making new friends, developing positive relationships with family members, and getting involved in activities that maintain and enhance your self-esteem. (See Figure 1-3.)

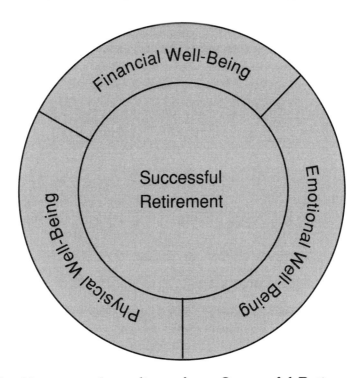

**The Necessary Ingredients for a Successful Retirement**
**Figure 1-3**

Your financial well being depends on your financial reserve, pension benefits and lifestyle needs. You can assess it by calculating a post-retirement budget. Consider your ability to fund that budget, taking into account the ravages of future inflation.

Your phsyical well being, to a large extent, depends on how well you have maintained your health, and your commitment to your future health. The Center for Disease Control reports that longevity is determined 25 percent by heredity and 75 percent by life style and environment. Clearly, you can make a difference.

The program presented in subsequent chapters focuses on your emotional well being. Crisp books that cover your financial and physical well being include:

*Personal Financial Fitness* by Allen Klosowski is very readable and effective for personal financial planning.

*Personal Wellness* by Rick Griggs teaches the basics of healthy living.

The best is *Comfort Zones* by Elwood Chapman, a comprehensive book on retirement planning.

All books can be purchased at your local bookstore or ordered directly from Crisp Publications, Inc., Menlo Park, California.

## RETIREMENT AND AGING

An important, basic area for emotional adjustment deals with your attitudes toward aging. You need to face your mortality, while recognizing the years of opportunity that lie ahead. Mr. E. L. Stephenson of Springdale, Arkansas is a good example of someone who worked through these issues. His story was reported on October 9, 1989, in the *Northwest Arkansas Times,* when he was 89 years old.

Aging is negative and dark and silly, he said, adding that he adamantly refuses to be put out to pasture. He describes people who "kill one another off" with negativity as "pimping for the undertaker."

When Stephenson retired, 20 years before, he bought an Airstream trailer to enjoy what he perceived to be the little time he had left. He even put it in his nephew's name to avoid probate. He did not want to admit he was negative, but at the time he remembers he was afraid to buy a green banana, fearing he would not be around when it ripened.

All that has changed. According to Stephenson, our lives begin at retirement. People are not old until they think they are old. "To hell with growing old!" he says.

Use this questionnaire to evaluate your attitude toward aging:

---

**Attitude Toward Aging**

Instructions: Mark each of the following statements either True or False.

|  | True | False |
|---|---|---|
| 1. Older people are out of touch with today's reality. | ____ | ____ |
| 2. No one has ever done anything worthwhile after age 75. | ____ | ____ |
| 3. Old age and dependency go hand-in-hand. | ____ | ____ |
| 4. Most older people live in the past. | ____ | ____ |
| 5. Most older people are cynical and boring. | ____ | ____ |
| 6. Older people find it difficult to learn new things. | ____ | ____ |
| 7. Most older people do not want to be productive. | ____ | ____ |
| 8. Creativity is a talent reserved for young people. | ____ | ____ |
| 9. There is nothing one can do after 65 to retain good health. | ____ | ____ |
| 10. Drivers over age 70 are a hazard to others. | ____ | ____ |

---

These statements are all "False." If you believe some of these statements to be true, you need to broaden your contacts with older people. Also, read the articles on aging that appear in your newspaper and subscribe to such magazines as *Modern Maturity, New Choices, Prime Time* and *Mature Outlook.*

## Fulfillment in Retirement

In recent years, aging in America has taken on new meaning. Older people find fulfillment in a wide range of endeavors, from helping others to pursuing their dreams of education, travel, the arts or entrepreneurial ventures. The following examples illustrate how some older people are spending their time today:

On April 1, 1991, the *Houston Chronicle* reported on Leola Kahrimanis, whose first novel *The Blue Hills Robbery,* was published when she was 86. Her adventure tale is based on what she imagined it would be like for two of her great-grandsons to explore the area where she lived as a child. Her book is being marketed to libraries and schools in Texas.

On September 8, 1991, *USA Weekend* reported on six active 90 + year olds, living life to its fullest. One, Rose Blumkin, age 97, works 12 to 14 hours a day operating *Mrs. B's Warehouse* in Omaha. She started the business after her two grandsons "ignored her in decision making and stifled her authority" in the business she and her late husband started in 1937.

Another, Noel Johnson, was 72 when his life insurance was canceled because he was such a bad risk. He was forty pounds overweight and suffered from high blood pressure, gout, arthritis, bursitis and a heart ailment. In his words, he was "smokin', drinking' and not takin' care of myself." Now, at 92, exercise and diet have erased years of physical atrophy. He ran his eighth marathon on November 3, 1991 and looked forward to being the first 100 year old to run the New York City Marathon. He said he was glad to be 92 years young, rather than 70 years old.

Clearly, you can continue to be productive, creative, and grow intellectually as long as you choose.

## The Retirement Years

The retirement years can be separated into three major periods. The timing of each period varies considerably based on individual health. However, for the majority of people, the breakdown in Figure 1-4 will be fairly accurate.

Period 1: Window of Opportunity: Retirement to late 70s

Period 2: Slowing Down: Late 70s to mid 80s

Period 3: Assisted Living: Mid 80s on

**Three Major Periods of Later Life**
**Figure 1-4**

The *Window of Opportunity* is best described as continuing to enjoy about the same health you have been experiencing, and having a high level of interest in doing things.

The *Slowing Down* period is characterized by the onset of physical limitations. The muscles and joints may not work as well as in the past, particularly if you have neglected your diet and exercise. Eyesight and hearing may deteriorate. You will continue to enjoy the same things as in the past, but it will take longer to do them. As a result, you will probably give up some of your more physically demanding activities.

The *Assisted Living* period is characterized by the need for help with the chores of daily living. Needs may include household chores, personal care and grooming or health care. Remember that 42 percent of the population over 85 today live independently; 25 percent receive some assistance, but still live in their own homes; and only 33 percent live in nursing homes or other care facilities.

## CONCLUSION

Your retirement can be the most enjoyable period of your life. If you have a secure financial base and reasonably good health, you can turn your attention to your emotional adjustment to retirement. Moving from the comfortable environment of work to a similarly comfortable environment in retirement will take some adjustment. It may take a couple of years of your time, but the effort you put into the transition will be well worthwhile.

Two principles will help you. First, have realistic expectations: consider your own personal limitations and take them into account. Second, have a positive outlook: your attitude will strongly influence your experience, so go into retirement—and old age—expecting the most. Then, work to see that you are not disappointed.

# Chapter 2

# *The Importance of Work*

Work is a significant part of most people's lives. When retirement is equated to not working, it suggests a great void during the retirement years. Of course, there are aspects of work that everyone looks forward to giving up. But, on balance, work is an enjoyable experience for most people. It is this significance of work in your life that makes the transition to retirement so challenging.

## WORK'S CONTRIBUTIONS

To carry out a successful transition, you need to understand the importance of work in your life and consider alternative sources for replacing the contributions that work has made. Figure 2-1 summarizes generally accepted contributions from work:

> - Income
> - Structure
> - Identity
> - Social Contract
> - Psychological Needs Satisfaction

**Contributions from Work**
**Figure 2-1**

## Income

Work is a source of income. The need for income is the first and foremost reason people seek work. Only after this need is satisfied can people direct their attention to other benefits from working.

With retirement, there is less need for income. At this point, the cost of educating children has usually been met, the home mortgage has been paid off, and daily living expenses are less. Expenses associated with working are no longer a part of the family budget. Complementing this need for less are income items that come with retirement—IRA's, pensions, Social Security and organization-sponsored, as well as personal, savings. When you compare your income and expenses, you may find that you no longer need to work to generate income.

If your retirement income does not meet your needs, you may find it necessary to seek part-time work. Also, your activities—such as consulting, writing, teaching, and operating your own business may generate income as an ancillary benefit. How you can get involved in these activities will be discussed later. For now, consider your need for earned income and some possible activities you might choose to pursue:

---

I expect I will need to continue earning income following my retirement.     _____ Yes     _____ No

If you answered yes, check off some possible activities you would pursue:

_____ Get a part-time job.

_____ Get a full-time job.

_____ Become a consultant.

_____ Convert a hobby to a business.

_____ Become a teacher.

_____ Start my own business.

_____ Join the Peace Corps.

_____ Become a writer, artist, etc.

_____ Run for political office.

_____ Go to work for a charitable organization.

## Structure

Work structures your time. You have to rise early enough to get to work on time. Days off, holidays and vacations are set by your work schedule. You must be certain places at certain times.

Many people look forward to retirement as becoming free from the structure imposed by their work schedules. Others, however, feel a loss when they give up their familiar routines.

When you leave work, you will need to consider your daily routine. Many people find some structure necessary, but prefer it to be less routine than when they were working. What time will you rise? When will you go to bed? Do you prefer to read a morning or afternoon newspaper? When will you eat your meals? What organizations will you be active in and when do they meet? Talking through these questions with your spouse or a close friend will help clarify the amount of structure appropriate for your life. Your answers to the following questions will also help you clarify your need for structure:

Select one statement from each pair:

1. _____ I feel a need to accomplish something each week.
   _____ As long as I enjoy what I am doing, it does not matter to me whether or not I accomplish anything.

2. _____ I am more comfortable on a regular schedule.
   _____ A regular schedule is unimportant to me. I do things whenever I feel like doing them.

3. _____ I prefer to plan things several days ahead.
   _____ I enjoy spur of the moment activities.

4. _____ I am most comfortable in an orderly environment.
   _____ I am not bothered by disarray.

5. _____ I like to know who is in charge and what lines of authority exist.
   _____ I prefer situations where no one is in charge—everyone pitches in and does what is needed.

Results: The first statement in each set reflects a need for structure, while the second statement reflects a preference for no structure. Most people fall somewhere between these two extremes.

What do your responses tell you about your need for structure? _____

### Identity

Most people identify closely with their profession or trade and employer. What you do for a living often is the topic of casual conversations. Facing your identity, beyond your career, is one of the major challenges for retirees. How will you answer the question, "What do you do?" after you retire?

There are two major alternatives. One is to continue to identify with your work and prior employer, and add *retired* to your status. For example, people frequently say, "I am a retired school teacher" or, "I am a retired engineer for the XYZ Company." The other alternative is to identify with some new endeavor.

The first alternative looks to the past and suggests that you are doing nothing now. Being a retired school teacher is not doing anything today. It says only what you did in the past. Sort through your life and find some current activities you can identify with today. When someone asks you what you do, be prepared to respond. The following list offers some possibilities. Check those that apply to you:

_____ 1. Hobbies and crafts such as needlework, woodworking, photography and collecting

_____ 2. Leisure activities such as golfing, hunting, fishing, traveling and attending cultural events

_____ 3. Community activities such as serving on boards, committees, commissions, etc., elected offices, volunteer fire fighters and emergency service corps

_____ 4. Fraternal and service organizations such as Moose, Elks, Kiwanis, Lions, Rotary, Optimists and Oddfellows

_____ 5. Political activities on behalf of the party or cause of your choice

_____ 6. Volunteer activities with churches, schools or charitable agencies

_____ 7. Continued active involvement with your professional or trade society

_____ 8. Educational activities

_____ 9. Activities promoting development and pride in your community such as the Chamber of Commerce and city beautification projects

_____ 10. Family centered activities such as organizing a reunion, grandparenting, and caring for a family member in need

From this list you will probably find several things that you currently do you will continue to do in retirement. So, when someone asks you what you do, rather than saying "Nothing," you can say, for example, you do a number of things including serving as a volunteer, playing golf and collecting antique piggy banks.

## Social Contact

A very significant part of the work experience is the friendships that develop from close association over long periods of time. These friendships become one of the major casualties of retirement. If you have social contact with colleagues outside the workplace, you can expect these friendships to continue. However, if you only see people at work, you can expect these relationships to end with your retirement. Rarely do friendships that are limited to work grow stronger with retirement. You simply do not have the opportunity to get together. This is often because the things you share are work-related. Single people who have not developed a social life beyond the workplace find this a particularly frightening prospect.

Complete the following exercise on page 18 to gauge the impact of your retirement on your social system.

## Social System Exercise

Instructions: List members of your social system in their proper category. Consider friends with whom you socialize, engage in recreational activities, share personal problems, concerns, feelings, etc. Rate each relationship as either "1" intimate, "2" close, or "3" casual. In the left margin, check those relationships you expect will continue beyond retirement.

| Friends at Work | Rating | Other Friends | Rating |
|---|---|---|---|
|  |  |  |  |
|  |  |  |  |
|  |  |  |  |
|  |  |  |  |
|  |  |  |  |
|  |  |  |  |
|  |  |  |  |
|  |  |  |  |
|  |  |  |  |

Generally, people who have several friends outside of work will find the transition easier because their social support will continue. If most of your friendships are limited to work, you will experience a greater loss at retirement.

The process to develop or expand your social support system after retirement is very similar to when you moved to a new community earlier in life. First, get out and make contact with others. Choose organizations where you expect to find people with interests similar to yours. Second, be a friend by offering to be of service, inviting people to join you in some activity, sharing your time and talent. Finally, remember that it takes time for friendships to develop—do not be too anxious.

What does this tell you about the need to maintain your social support system by working to keep existing friendships and to develop new ones?

_____

_____

_____

_____

_____

_____

_____

## Psychological Needs Satisfaction

A feeling of self-worth is important for good mental health. Many people get that feeling through their work. They contribute and receive feedback that confirms and bolsters their self-esteem. Retirement destroys this system. How will you go about building a new system to provide you with a sense of purpose and an opportunity for self-expression, accomplishment, growth and recognition?

Some people think their needs will change with retirement. They look forward to less pressure from their jobs and opportunities to relax. But, they are bored after a month or so of retirement. During the early months they may feel lost in memories of how it used to be. They may not have a clear perception of how to direct their creative energies. The fact is you are the same person on the first day of retirement as you were on the last day of work. You have the same needs. The same things turn you on and off. Without an alternative to satisfy your needs, you will become frustrated and depressed.

Complete the following exercise to understand what is important to you. It will also help you see whether your life is focused narrowly on work.

---

**Needs Satisfaction Exercise**

*Instructions:* Rate the importance to you of the following common psychological needs. Use "1" to indicate very important, "2" moderately important, "3" somewhat important. Do not rate any you consider unimportant. For those rated, allocate 100% between on the job and off the job to show how those needs are currently being satisfied.

| Need | Rating | Currently Satisfied | |
|------|--------|-----------|-----------|
|      |        | On the Job | Off the Job |
| Achieving goals | | | |
| Being recognized for achievements | | | |
| Belonging to a group | | | |
| Making things happen | | | |
| Having a sense of purpose | | | |
| Continuing to grow mentally | | | |
| Creating new things | | | |
| Experiencing new adventures | | | |
| Making a contribution | | | |
| Having leadership responsibilities | | | |

Generally, people who experience a good deal of needs satisfaction from non-work related activities will transition more easily into retirement. They will continue in activities they find satisfying. However, if all or most of their needs satisfaction comes from work, their transition to retirement will be more difficult. They will need to seek out and get involved in activities that will provide them with satisfaction they no longer experience from work. Alternative activities will be summarized in later chapters.

How will you fulfill your needs and maintain your self-esteem in retirement?

_____

_____

_____

_____

_____

_____

_____

_____

_____

_____

_____

## CONCLUSION

While most people look forward to getting away from the job, in reality work is a very important part of life. People miss it after retirement. All too often, people appreciate the economic gains from work and overlook the social and psychological ones. These social and psychological benefits are missed most.

Planning a successful transition requires you to be completely honest with the significance of work in your life. This includes acknowledging the structure, identity, social contact and psychological needs satisfaction that work provides. When work is no longer your major endeavor, seek out ways to replace the contribution that it makes to your life.

Alternatives to full-time work are nearly limitless. You can choose among leisure activities, educational activities, volunteer service activities or activities that generate income. Among these choices you surely will find the right combination for you.

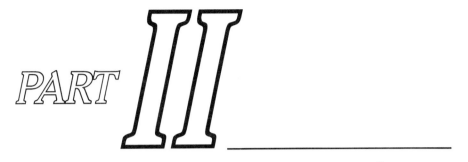

# PART II

## Making the Transition

# Chapter 3

# *The Transition Experience*

To properly prepare for your transition to retirement, it will help to understand what to expect. Four phases of transition will be described in this chapter. Also, negative emotions evoked by the transition experience will be explored. In chapters four and five, the transition experience will be examined in the context of work and home.

## THE FOUR PHASES OF TRANSITION

Some people view retirement as a single event that occurs on a specific date. Everything before that date is career; everything after it is retirement. This is a narrow view of the experience. Just as marriage is preceded by courtship, retirement needs to be preceded by a period of emotional and practical preparation.

Successful retirement involves a four phase transition, which begins long before the final day on the job. An orderly process provides the proper framework for working through the emotional turmoil triggered by approaching retirement. The transition is a gradual slowing down at work as you shift emotionally from career priorities to personal priorities. Planning and following the transition will keep you in control of your future, alert you to what lies ahead, and help you avoid the pitfalls that keep many retirees from finding their post-career niche.

## Acknowledgment

The first phase of your transition, Acknowledgment, is gaining a concrete understanding that you will retire. You may not have set a retirement date, but you acknowledge you will not work forever. Everyone has to face this phase. Unfortunately, many people avoid acknowledging the reality of their retirement until it is too late to do anything about it.

Acknowledgment should begin three to five years before you retire. This provides an opportunity to think about retirement, well in advance of the actual date. During this time, you can honestly assess your career and future. At home with your family you can begin talking about the future. These assessments and discussions will arouse a variety of reactions to the prospects of retiring. Some will be emotional; others will be practical. With these reactions aroused, you will be motivated to resolve them. This moves you into the next phase of transition.

## Acceptance

Acceptance involves dealing with and resolving the reactions experienced in the Acknowledgment phase. During the Acceptance phase, you will come to terms with what your career has meant to you and begin planning for life after your career. During this phase, involvement and support from family members becomes increasingly important.

After you acknowledge that you will retire, you may find yourself experiencing several negative emotions. You may find it difficult to accept leaving friends and familiar surroundings to move into an unknown future. These feelings can be very disturbing. And, when you experience them, it is important *not* to ignore them or avoid dealing with them. Do not expect to solve these problems overnight. Some of the more troubling issues may be with you for some time.

Your emotional reaction to pending retirement will be counterbalanced by your practical reaction. The reality of retirement is significant enough to encourage you to plan for it. Making specific plans about when you will retire, where you will live after retirement, and what you will do will help you deal with the emotional turmoil of Acceptance. You will feel much more positive and in control if you start taking steps now to plan making realistic plans, you will remain mired in the past. Those who cannot "accept" retirement emotionally, find themselves in a situation they are unable to reverse and unable to reconcile.

## Disengagement

Acknowledgment and Acceptance are basically mental exercises. They prepare you mentally for the future, while you are still fully involved with your career. Disengagement brings action to your retirement transition. During this phase, there is a reduction in the emotional involvement with your career and a selective reduction in the actual work. This phase is vitally important to both you and your organization. During this time, you make sure others are trained to carry on after your departure. During this phase you should also identify the select few achievements you want to complete before you leave.

At home, you will increase your effort in testing out your post-career lifestyle and activities. You will increase your involvement with post-career social and organizational networks. You will continue to involve your family members in planning and decision making, at least to the extent that they will be affected.

Disengagement should begin one to two years before you retire. The steps you take during this phase will help you deal with any remaining Acceptance issues. A successful Disengagement weans you from emotional dependency on your career and lays out a path to retirement. It puts a cap on your career, leaving you free to move on to the next stage of your life.

## Redefinition

Redefinition begins after you retire. It marks the start of a rewarding post-career life, beginning immediately after the retirement party and post-career vacation. Any remaining career-related issues are resolved and are replaced by concerns about achieving post-career goals. You will finalize the plans you made before retirement and begin to put them into practice. As you find your niche in retirement, you will set in motion the process of building a comfortable set of circumstances for yourself. This is when you might relocate, or become seriously involved in volunteer, hobby, leisure or educational activities. You will become comfortable knowing your career is a completed chapter of your life and you will be busy writing the next one. This phase may take up to two years. If you neglect it, you may find your thoughts dwelling on missed opportunities and career disappointments, and never complete your transition.

## THE NEGATIVE EMOTIONS OF RETIREMENT

Everyone responds differently to retirement. Not all reactions are negative, but, be prepared to deal with some negative emotions as you go through your retirement transition. They will most likely appear, since they are a normal part of the experience. Your goal will be to work through them, rather than let them slow you down.

Feeling grief-stricken, rejected, angry or fearful does not mean you have an emotional problem. These natural reactions to the disturbing issues of retirement need to be experienced to be resolved. The real problems begin when these emotions are ignored or underestimated.

Depression is the most common result of not dealing properly with these emotions. This is usually the first sign that someone is having difficulty making an effective transition. You can avoid this, and similar problems, by working through each of the phases of transition.

### Grief

Grief is most common during the later stages of Disengagement and during Redefinition. This is when you come face-to-face with the fact that your career is over. As you take stock of your career and life, many aspects will be tinged with grief. Knowing that they can never be relived, even memories of good times may make you feel sad.

Along with the promise that retirement holds, it is also a time of letting go, of leaving behind things that have had great meaning and personal importance for a significant part of your life. Friendships are severed, dreams of career possibilities will never be realized, triumphs will never to be repeated. Saying goodbye creates grief, a feeling of loss or disconnectedness, of mourning.

Grief is a normal and healthy reaction to retirement. Experiencing it leads to a catharsis that helps you resolve your feelings about your career and allows you to move freely into the future.

## Rejection

Feelings of being unwanted, unneeded and unloved can be part of the retirement experience. Even organizational efforts to help someone prepare for retirement can be seen through a veil of rejection.

Those who look for rejection are often looking for signals to confirm subconscious feelings about themselves. Times of emotional vulnerability are when you are most prone to these feelings. Rejection, like fear, can be a paralyzing emotion. However, rather than being threatened from the outside, you feel worthless from the inside. Be prepared to handle three potential areas of rejection.

*Professional Rejection:* Those who feel victimized by retirement may look for signs that others are glad to see them go. You may see rejection in procedural changes from the way you did things, or in suggestions or ideas of yours that are not adopted. Your reactions to these and other experiences may turn your suspicion of rejection into a self-fulfilling prophecy.

*Personal Rejection:* As retirement approaches, if you feel unwanted and unneeded at work, you may look for similar signals in your personal life. Retirement can be a time of extreme emotional vulnerability. You may be looking for any thread of evidence to prove that it will be every bit as bad as you thought it would be, and you may be on the lookout for any treatment that will reinforce your feelings of rejection.

*Internal Rejection:* Feelings of internal rejection are often projections of uncertainty about your future role. Clearcut roles at work and at home will change with retirement. You may reject yourself, or feel worthless, when you no longer fill the position of breadwinner at home and whatever your position was at work.

## Fear

Change, even for the better, provokes stress and anxiety. And retirement ranks in the top 10 of life's most stress-producing events. The stress and anxiety retirement provokes can reach the level of fear.

Fear can immobilize or create confusion. It tends to occupy the mind to the exclusion of other emotions, particularly pleasure and optimism. Allowing fear to take over prevents the possibility of approaching the future with confidence. You may be particularly sensitive to five potentional areas of fear:

***Fear of the Unknown:*** Work has a reassuring degree of structure and familiarity. Retirement raises questions of what lies ahead and your ability to meet the associated challenges.

***Fear of Loss of Identity:*** Many people see themselves only as the roles dictated by their careers. Subconsciously, they may feel they will cease to exist after retirement. They fear becoming "no one" after being stripped of their position in the organization.

***Fear of Loss of Power:*** At work, people are able to make things happen. This power is lost in retirement and the subliminal message of impotency can be terrifying.

***Fear of Financial Need:*** Even those most financially secure worry about money. During your career, if you have equated work with pay, you may subconsciously believe that without work, there will be no money. These thoughts foster crippling attitudes about personal finances.

***Fear of Aging and Mortality:*** Retirement sends a strong message that you are getting older. The tendency is to think that the best is over and to become despondent. In the extreme, this fear can be a self-fulfilling prophecy. Some people shut themselves off from life, "waiting for the end" rather than taking control of their post-career lives.

## Anger

Anger is a typical response to retirement. You do not have to face forced retirement to feel angry about leaving. Anger displaces the frustration and resentment you may feel. Ultimately, it can divert you from dealing with retirement planning and can interfere with sound decision-making. Anger takes a variety of forms and can be pointed in many different directions. Here are five to watch for:

***Anger at the Organization:*** You may feel forced out or upset that you were not given enough notice, properly prepared, or given alternatives. As a result, the organization becomes an obvious place to direct your anger.

*Anger at Others:* Feelings that co-workers or family do not appreciate change that you are undergoing can trigger irrational anger. Even if others do not do anything, general unhappiness and dissatisfaction with the prospect of retirement can emerge as anger directed at those closest to you.

*Anger at Specific Individuals:* Rivals, subordinates and superiors with whom you have not always seen eye-to-eye may provoke anger and precipitate quarrels.

*Anger at Self:* This anger exhibits itself most strongly after retirement. You may become angry at yourself if you have not properly planned and prepared for retirement.

*Displaced Anger:* Anger is often directed at inanimate objects. You may become short-tempered and easily riled. The anger inside you may come out when the desk drawer will not open or the computer will not do what you want. Small frustations you once handled without difficulty may become triggers of emotional outbursts.

## Guilt

Feelings of guilt are experienced when you reflect on something you should or should not have done. You may feel guilty that you did not plan and save sufficiently for your retirement, so that your spouse and/or family could enjoy the retirement and inheritance you feel they are entitled to. You may feel guilty over some past action at work toward a fellow worker or supervisor. Or, you may feel guilty over work left undone.

While not experienced by everyone, guilt may be a part of your feelings about retirement. If so, the best way to deal with it is to accept your responsibility for your past action (or inaction) and change those things that can be changed. Begin immediately to plan your future. As a part of your disengagement, address relationships that need attention and handle any unfinished projects before you leave. Take whatever action is required to resolve your feelings of guilt and move forward with a clear conscience.

## CONCLUSION

The transition to retirement can be an emotionally-charged experience. Not everyone will feel the same emotions. To some extent, it will depend upon the circumstances surrounding your retirement—did you freely elect to retire, or was it forced upon you due to staff reduction, reorganization or ill health? Even under the best of circumstances, you will feel some grief over leaving familiar surroundings and people that were important in your work life. Also, there will likely be some fear of the unknown that lies ahead.

The four phases of transition to retirement will help you deal with these emotions, as well as with the practical realities of change. During Acknowledgment, you come to grips emotionally with retirement as a reality in your future. You honestly assess your current position and future prospects. During this process, you may decide that, in the future, you want to focus your energy on other areas of life. Retirement will afford you that opportunity.

Acceptance requires you to work through the emotions evoked by retirement and actively plan when you will retire, where you will live and what you will do. As you deal with these practical issues a clearer picture of your future begins to emerge and the emotions will dissipate.

Disengagement is a vital part of the process, for you and the organization. Emotionally and physically, you become less involved in the actual work as you prepare the organization to carry on without you. You should have two objectives during this phase: to see that others know everything about your job and how to do it, and to complete the few tasks that will bring closure for you.

Redefinition occurs after retirement. It involves moving to a new set of comfortable circumstances. This could include relocation and definitely involves finding your niche in volunteer, educational, hobby or leisure activities.

The four phases of transition do not exist in isolation. They often overlap. Issues you felt were resolved in one phase may reoccur much later. However, as long as you concentrate on going through the phases, one at a time, you will follow a path that will minimize emotional problems and maximize satisfaction in retirement.

# Chapter 4

# *The Transition at Work*

Retirement can be forced upon you by ill health or workforce reduction. Either of these circumstances will alter your transition experience. Your feelings will be different, and typically, you will have less time to adjust to the notion of retirement and to deal with the practical matters surrounding it.

Retirement can be chosen freely. This, of course, is most desirable. Since it allows for an orderly transition—you choose retirement on your own terms. Generally, three criteria define how long someone may work:

- Your job is necessary to your employer

- Your performance is satisfactory and

- You choose to continue working

With the exception of a few governmental careers and airline pilots, age is no longer a determining factor in retirement decisions. Everyone else can continue working as long as these three criteria are met. This point was emphasized by an Associated Press article in the Springdale, AR *Morning News* on September 22, 1992. The article announced the retirement of Steve Minnich of Beltsville, MD on August 31, 1992 at age 98. Until his retirement, he worked eight hours each day as a heating and cooling equipment salesman. When asked why he had not retired sooner, he said he liked meeting people and his work gave him that opportunity.

## THREE PHASES OF THE TRANSITION

Transition at work involves three of the four phases—acknowledgment, acceptance and disengagement. The fourth phase, redefinition, takes place after you leave your job. If you choose freely to retire, your transition can be at a more leisurely pace than if you are forced to retire. In both cases, all four phases must be experienced and resolved.

### Acknowledgment

One of the definitions of retirement mentioned in Chapter 1 is: "Leaving the organization after qualifying for immediate pension benefits." As you approach the time when you become eligible for immediate pension benefits, you begin to realize that retirement is an option. You may choose to continue working or not. As long as it is at least three years away, *this* is the time to begin thinking about retirement. Your actual retirement date may be several years away; acknowledging that your career could be drawing to a close signals the beginning of your transition.

At this point, there are several things you can do to help you acknowledge the reality of pending retirement:

- Honestly assess your career. How satisfying is the work you are doing? What are your prospects for the future?

- Study the details of your organization's retirement plans. Get an estimate of your benefits.

- Calculate your net additional income from working, compared to retiring. (Use the worksheet in this chapter.)

- Visit with three or four close friends who are about to retire or who recently retired.

- If your organization offers them, attend a retirement planning seminar.

- Meet with a financial planner and design a plan to meet your financial needs in retirement.

- Organize a retirement resources file. Make individual folders for topics important to planning your future—such as housing, location, health and well being, and activities.

- Determine what you want out of life, and write down your life goals. Involve others who might be affected by your decisions.

***The Economics of Working versus Retiring:*** Generally, you will have more income while working. It is important to know how much income you will have after taxes and work related expenses are taken into account. You may be surprised. Use this worksheet to get an idea of the difference:

| | Working | Retired |
|---|---|---|
| **Income** | | |
| Salary & Bonus | | |
| Pension | | |
| IRA Income | | |
| 401(k) Income | | |
| Savings Plan Income | | |
| Social Security | | |
| Other Income | | |
| **Taxes** | | |
| Federal Income | | |
| State Income | | |
| Social Security | | |
| **Work Related Expenses** | | |
| Commuting | | |
| Meals | | |
| Clothing | | |
| Laundry & Dry Cleaning | | |
| After Tax Net Income | | |
| **Marginal Net Income from Working** | | |

*Retirement Gains and Losses:* The worksheet summarizing your net income before and after retiring focused your attention on the financial gains and losses with retirement. Retirement involves more than just finances.

As you contemplate retirement, you are likely to be pulled between the attraction of working and the attraction of retiring. Each will have positive features. At the same time, you may associate some negative features with each. To help you assess the impact of retirement on your life, complete the following exercise.

---

### Gains and Losses with Retirement

*Instructions:* List gains you associate with retirement. For example: more free time, less stress and more control over your schedule. Next, list losses you associate with retirement, such as enjoyment of the work, association with colleagues, and positive feedback for accomplishments. Note: If you are married, have your spouse complete the exercise, then discuss each other's responses.

| Gains | Losses |
|-------|--------|
| _____ | _____ |
| _____ | _____ |
| _____ | _____ |
| _____ | _____ |
| _____ | _____ |
| _____ | _____ |
| _____ | _____ |

*Retirement Concerns:* As you contemplate change in your life, you will have many unanswered questions or concerns. This is natural at this point in your transition. Write down your concerns; this will help you identify for yourself the things you must deal with in the next phase. The following exercise will help you identify your concerns:

---

**Concerns About Retirement**

*Instructions:* List all concerns you have about your retirement. These might include such things as the effects of inflation on your expenses, care of your parents, where you will live, and how you will spend your time. Note: If you are married, also have your spouse complete the exercise; then discuss each other's responses.

_____

_____

_____

_____

_____

_____

_____

---

## Acceptance

As you move from Acknowledgment to Acceptance, you will begin the work of actually preparing for your retirement. At this point, you are probably still two to three years away from the actual date. During this phase, you will address the concerns you have identified about retirement. You will begin to find answers. Begin to experiment with post-career lifestyles and emotionally disengage from your work.

During this phase you will also deal with your unwarranted fears and doubts about retirement. Continue gathering information in your Retirement Resources File and take more active steps in planning your future.

***Your Retirement Date:*** Setting the date of your retirement is an important decision that will become the core of your planning. During Acknowledgment you plan in a general way. Now your plans become more specific. Although some people are quite comfortable tying their retirement to attaining a certain age or completing a targeted number of years with their organization, it is best not to think of retirement as an arbitrary age or date. The following factors will help you with your decision. Consider each of them carefully as you make your final decision.

- *Organizational Practices:* Ask when is the best time during the year to retire from your organization. How is accrued vacation handled? How are age and service rounded for pension calculation?

- *Project Completion:* Are you working on a major project? Would it be practical to retire when it is finished, rather than starting something new?

- *Reorganization:* Is your group or department planning to reorganize? Would it be practical to let someone else handle the reorganization?

- *Career Prospects:* What are your prospects for the future? How rewarding is your present work?

- *Family Responsibilities:* Are your children reared and educated? Many people tie retirement to the last child becoming independent.

- *Financial Status:* Can you afford to retire? Often retirement is planned to coincide with making the last mortgage payment on a home.

- *Health:* What is the status of your health? Is your job physically strenuous? Or, do you enjoy good health and want to retire while you can do some of the things you have looked forward to?

- *Alternative Activities:* Do you have alternative activities to occupy your time and satisfy your psychological needs?

To help you assess retirement readiness, write a brief assessment of each of the following issues. Then, using the information you have written, complete the "Focusing In On Retirement" questionnaire.

Health: _____

_____

_____

_____

Family Responsibilities: _____

_____

_____

_____

Career: _____

_____

_____

_____

Alternative Activities: _____

_____

_____

_____

Financial Status: _____

_____

_____

_____

**Focusing On Retirement**

1. Given my age and service with the organization, the earliest I can retire and receive pension benefits immediately is:

   _____

2. At the present time I plan to work until: _____
   (date)

3. The reason I picked this date is: _____

   _____

   _____

   _____

4. The reason I plan to retire is: _____

   _____

   _____

   _____

5. In retirement, I expect my life to be different in the following ways:

   _____

   _____

   _____

6. What do close family members think about my retirement plans?

   _____

   _____

   _____

*Life Beyond Career:* A part of the Acceptance phase is to begin to define yourself as a person in non-work-related terms. Nearly everyone fills several roles in life. Some are work-related, such as supervisor, technician, nurse or manager. Others, such as parent, spouse, golfer, church member and taxpayer, are non-work-related. The following exercise will help you sort through the various roles you fill today and what your life will be like in retirement:

---

1. List all the roles you fill today.

_____          _____

_____          _____

_____          _____

_____          _____

_____          _____

_____          _____

_____          _____

_____          _____

_____          _____

2. Cross out those roles that will disappear when you retire.

---

You will probably find that most of your roles remain after retirement. Those that remain are of greatest significance. What are you doing to develop them? What could you do to make them better? What other roles would you like to add to your life in retirement?

Using the information and insight you gained from this exercise, without referring to your career, write a summary of who you are.

_____

_____

_____

_____

_____

_____

_____

_____

_____

_____

## Disengagement

By this time, you should have definite plans of when you will retire and what you expect to do in retirement. Disengagement is the process of both physically and emotionally weaning yourself from your career. Typically it will take one to two years to complete.

During the Disengagement phase, you will want to see that someone is trained to handle all of the work you have been doing, complete any pending projects that will bring closure to your career, and reduce the amount of time you spend on the job. Also, details of your retirement announcement, celebration and exit will need to be handled.

***Turning Your Work Over to Others:*** Most people feel an obligation to their organization to see that their work will continue to be done after they are gone. Depending on the training involved, you may need to begin the process before you are prepared to announce your retirement. If so, develop a story to justify your action, such as, "You never know when illness or injury will strike, so it's important that someone else knows how to handle this work."

Begin by identifying work you handle personally that no one else can do. Identify staff members who could be trained to handle that work. If necessary, obtain your supervisor's or manager's approval before starting the training. The following worksheet will help:

| Work I Am Doing Today | To Be Trained |
|---|---|
| | |
| | |
| | |
| | |
| | |
| | |
| | |
| | |

*Projects To Be Completed:* As your career comes to a close, you may want to complete a few projects you have been working on. This will include projects that you have proposed or initiated that will bring you recognition, allowing you to retire on a high. It also will include projects that would be difficult to hand over to a successor because of their complexity. Finally, consider projects that you are committed to but believe it is unlikely that someone else would be as committed to as you are; if you do not complete them, they will not get done, or at least not to your standards.

| Projects To Be Completed | Target Completion Date |
|---|---|
|  |  |
|  |  |
|  |  |
|  |  |
|  |  |
|  |  |
|  |  |
|  |  |
|  |  |
|  |  |

If you have supervisory and/or managerial responsibilities, you need to be sensitive to your staff's needs during their transition to your successor. You may be required to attend to various administrative matters affecting them, such as performance assessments, salary increase forecasts, vacation schedules and budgets.

*Tapering Off:* During the last six to twelve months, you should taper off on the hours you work. As you train others to handle work you are presently doing, you may be able to turn some of it over to them. This will free up your time. If you work evening and/or weekends, cut back on or eliminate these out-of-schedule hours. Often, the time at work can be spent more efficiently or certain work can be eliminated. This reduction in hours spent working will help you reduce your emotional involvement in the work. As you make more personal time available, you can begin to get involved in post-career activities. This will permit a shifting of emotional investment from work to other activities.

*Announcing Your Retirement:* To plan an orderly succession, your organization's management needs to know sufficiently in advance of your plans to retire. Your organization will have some bearing on the amount of time required to select and train your replacement. The average amount of notice is six months, within a range of two to twelve months. In the announcement memo to your management, limit your message to the facts of your planned departure. Avoid any temptation to critique the organization or its management. Remember, written documents can stay in files a long time.

Your retirement should be publicly announced one to two months before your departure. If the word gets out too early, you may be excluded from decisions that you typically participate in and you will spend a good deal of time discussing your plans. If you supervise a staff, personally advise them of your plans a day or two prior to any public announcement.

*Your Retirement Party:* Virtually every organization holds a gathering to launch their members into retirement. Gatherings vary considerably, from a formal dinner to punch and cookies at the office. These affairs are important; they serve the emotional needs of those you leave behind, as well as your own. Colleagues and staff need to adjust to your leaving. Depending on your relationship with them and your impact on the organization, these needs can be strong.

Discuss the kind of send-off you will be given. Take part in planning the kind of gathering you will be comfortable with. Of course, you have the option of refusing this kind of gathering. If you do, understand your reasons. Is it because you cannot face retirement? Have you not completely accepted it? As an alternative to your organization's traditional farewell, consider a lunch with a few close colleagues and staff.

To prepare yourself emotionally to participate in your retirement party, complete the following questions:

1) List five turning points in your career.

    _____    _____

    _____    _____

    _____    _____

2) List your five greatest career disappointments.

3) What unique contributions have you made to the organization?

4) Incorporate this information into a write-up of what your career has meant to you.

*Cleaning Out Your Work Area:* Cleaning out your work area can be a melancholy experience. You can reduce the impact by starting well in advance of your last day. Start by removing a few non-essential things such as books, pictures and mementos. As time permits, go through files and get rid of unnecessary items. This process helps you disengage yourself from your career, and prevents the air of finality that goes with a massive one-day move out.

Save personal mementos, but avoid taking boxes of useless correspondence home that will be in your way and take up space. If you cannot face throwing something away, give it to someone else at work.

*Your Last Day at Work:* Your last day on the payroll is typically dictated by policy. If you have accrued leave, you may elect to take off work several days or weeks before your actual retirement. If you have taken vacation at a certain time for several years, you could go on vacation and not return to work when it is over. Some people find it comfortable to work up to the Christmas holiday and then not return to work. Pick a last day that is comfortable for both you and your management.

Your last day at work should be relatively free of work responsibilities. Your successor should be in place and able to handle the routine activities of the job. You should tend to any administrative matters, such as turning in your keys, identification card, credit cards and expense accounts. You may need to attend debriefing meetings and come to agreement on the use of proprietary information.

On your last day it would be appropriate to have lunch with two or three close colleagues. Also, you may want to visit with a few close associates to say goodbye. With everything handled, plan to go home an hour or two early.

## CONCLUSION

While not everyone will have the opportunity to take three to five years to handle a transition to retirement, all of the steps are important to successfully disengage, both physically and emotionally, from work. If any of the steps are omitted, you will feel a lingering lack of closure on your career that will prevent you from becoming fully involved in your post-career endeavors.

When you acknowledge retirement as a possible option in your future, you need to explore both the financial and non-financial gains and losses retirement represents. This exploration is likely to trigger a number of concerns you have about retirement. Write down these concerns. You may continue to work for several years, building a retirement resource file, but not taking steps toward closing out your career.

At some point, you will accept retirement as the course you have chosen in the foreseeable future. When this happens, you will begin to develop specific plans—when you will retire, where you will live, what you will do. This will require researching and reconciling the list of concerns developed in the first phase of your transition.

With your plans developed, you will begin to disengage from your job. Train others to handle the work you are doing, identify and complete those special projects that will bring closure to your career, and begin physically and emotionally tapering off. Finally, carefully plan your announcement, celebration and last day in the office. Just as you do, colleagues and staff have to deal with their emotional needs. To lessen the emotional impact of the task, start cleaning out your work area several weeks before your last day.

When these steps are properly handled, you can move into retirement feeling good about your career and looking forward to what lies ahead. You may still have some butterflies in your stomach, but they are normal. Do not try to minimize the challenge that lies ahead, but do not sell yourself short either. You are ready to face and conquer them.

_____

# Chapter 5

# *The Transition at Home*

Half of the stress of retirement comes from leaving work; the other half is from coming home. Contrary to what many people believe, the transition at home does not begin *after* the last day of work. Preparing for retirement at home should begin when your preparation for retirement at work begins. In fact, if family members are included in discussions and decisions from the beginning, the two transitions will flow together as a natural process.

There are major differences in the two transitions. At work, you reduce emotional commitment and involvement as you close out your career. At home, commitment increases, and you become more involved. Even if you plan a second career or other activities that will keep you away from home, you will experience a transition at home. Retirement creates a changing dynamic that affects everyone around you, regardless of your retirement choice. Everyone must recognize the changes and make accommodations.

## THE FOUR PHASES OF TRANSITION

All four phases of the retirement transition have a place at home. Acknowledgment, Acceptance, and Disengagement have at-home agendas corresponding to those at work. Redefinition, the last phase of transition, takes place at home *after* you leave work. While thoughts of retirement typically center on work, even greater attention needs to be given to what will happen at home.

## Acknowledgment

Acknowledgment fosters awareness of pending retirement and retirement issues to those close to you. Its goal is to open channels of communications and develop a common front for facing the future. Discussions during this phase can lay the foundation for long-term happiness and fulfillment.

From a career perspective, when you are contemplating retirement it is easy to become preoccupied with your own concerns. However, your retirement will have a profound impact on your spouse. This is something you must also address. To a lesser degree, other family members and friends you are closely involved with will also be affected.

Of course, not everyone is married and has a family, but everyone needs external support to assist with their adjustment to retirement. Close friends and relatives can often fill this need. Relationships with these people can change, just as with family members. Whether you have a family or not, it is important to maintain and strengthen a retirement support group and to consider the impact of your retirement on relationships with those closest to you.

*Relationship Assessment:* Your career has had a powerful impact on your family relationships. It is important to consider the effect. Your successful career may have added to an overall sense of well-being for family members, and contributed to a rewarding family life. Or, the demands of your career may have contributed to the breakup of your marriage. Work is sometimes used as an escape from an unhappy relationship, and is blamed for creating the problems it is used to escape from. An important part of Acknowledgment is to assess the impact of your career on your family life, and look ahead to the changes retirement will bring. The following activities will help you do that:

- Write a brief description of the relationship you have with each member of your family. Include an assessment of how your career has impacted the relationship and the effect you anticipate retirement will have on it. If problems exist in any of your relationships, what can you do to improve the situation?

- How comfortable are you discussing personal and career problems with your spouse? How closely will you discuss and agree upon post-career plans?

*Communication:* Communication serves two major functions. It facilitates the exchange of information and it is the vehicle for establishing and maintaining relationships. Many people downplay the importance of this second function. However, in the transition to retirement, maintaining at-home relationships becomes increasingly important.

At work you deal in facts. At home you must deal with feelings. Feelings cannot be swept aside while you develop retirement budgets and schedules. Dealing with feelings is a vital part of retirement. These suggestions will make communicating with family members easier:

- Ask others to tell you about their feelings and how your retirement may affect them.

- Express understanding and concern for others' feelings.

- Be open and honest about your own feelings, both with yourself and others close to you.

- Remember, there is no right or wrong when discussing feelings—they simply are.

- Be flexible and willing to compromise to accommodate the concerns of other family members.

- Be curious about other peoples' concerns. Try to understand the underlying reasons for their anxiety, rather than dismissing their comments as unimportant. Ask questions for clarification and repeat back what you hear, in your own words, for verification.

Your training on the job may have encouraged you to be guarded in conversation. Your emphasis may have been on getting others to talk while you listened and kept your emotions under control. If this has been your experience, you may have to retrain yourself to be more emotionally active. If you have trouble expressing feelings, start with inconsequential topics, such as an article from the newspaper that piques an emotional reaction.

**Communications Exercise**

Discuss the following topics with your spouse or close friend. Your objective during this exercise is to understand his or her ideas, feelings, concerns, etc. about your proposed retirement. Do not be concerned at this time about reconciling differences that you uncover.

• What does retirement mean to your spouse? For example: aging, freedom, opportunity, the end of the road, or time together.

• What are your spouse's greatest concerns about your retirement? For example, there will not be enough income to support your lifestyle, he or she will experience a loss of status, you will be underfoot all day, or there will be restrictions on his or her freedom.

• What does your spouse expect retirement to be like? What does he or she expect of you after you retire?

• What does your spouse see as the greatest gain to the family with your retirement? What is seen as the greatest loss?

***Time and Family Relationships:*** The average worker does not spend much time with family members—maybe four or five hours each evening—when not traveling—and a few hours on weekends. Sometimes, even when physically at home, attention is consumed by work related problems. Retirement will dramatically alter the amount and type of time you spend at home.

During Acknowledgment, start thinking about the reality of this extra time, and how it will be spent. Couples who are not prepared, especially if the retiree has nothing to do, very quickly get on each other's nerves.

**Use of Time Exercise**

Discuss the following topics with your spouse.

- Which of your spouse's present activities does he or she wish to continue after your retirement?

- What new activities is your spouse interested in pursuing?

- What activities will you engage in together after you retire?

- What activities will you engage in alone after you retire?

*Family Roles and Retirement:* Consider your home life and marital relationship when thinking about in-home role adaptation. Who is in charge of what? Typically, men handle car, yard and house maintenance. Women manage the household and handle child rearing. Two-career families adhere less to traditional roles, but role adaptation still evolves. With retirement and more available time, problems can emerge around who takes care of various household chores. There is no pat formula to resolve these problems. Some will interpret your getting involved as an invasion of their turf and will resent you for it. If you do not get involved, some will resent your extra time and your not lending a hand. It is vital to discuss and plan, well in advance for these changes.

**Role Clarification Exercise**

Discuss the following topics with your spouse. At this point, it is more important to understand each other's point of view than to reach agreement. There is plenty of time to work out differences.

- What chores do each of you identify as your responsibility?

- What chores would you like to swap with your spouse? For example, some couples take turns, week-to-week, being responsible for their evening meals.

- What chores could you do together? For example, gardening or house cleaning.

- Which of you handles the family finances? How can you educate the other one in this responsibility?

A further consideration to encourage sharing and swapping household roles is that it is very unlikely that both members of a couple will die at the same time. Therefore, one will be left to live alone. It is a commonly known fact that women fare better alone than men. One of several reasons for this is that women are skilled in managing the household. Men can easily learn these skills by working along with their wives.

***Relationships with Children:*** Relationships with children also change during the retirement transition. Your retirement is a clear example of their growing older. Most children will respond positively to their parent's retirement. They usually believe their parent has earned retirement through hard work and deserves a less demanding lifestyle. While they are supportive, they may be overly optimistic and take for granted financial security and emotional adjustments.

Adult children may begin to treat retired parents paternalisticly. They view retirement in the traditional and outdated way, as a time to take it easy—a signal of declining capabilities. This evolving relationship may trigger resentment in the parents. Potentially harmless jokes about being "over the hill" may hit home with more impact than intended.

***Other Considerations:*** There are more things to discuss at home than family members' reactions to your anticipated retirement. Your spouse, in particular, should be actively involved in helping formulate workable and realistic plans, including decisions about future housing needs, updating wills and insurance arrangements, and tax considerations.

Your home will become the headquarters for examining non-career issues. Begin your transition early and include your spouse as a full partner in the venture. This involvement will make your transition and retirement easier long before your career ends, and it will pay dividends in terms of a more rewarding home life.

### Acceptance

At work, Acceptance is a mental exercise and does not involve reduction in career involvement. At home, Acceptance includes active steps to prepare you and your family for the changes retirement will bring. Acceptance is the time you and your spouse assess mutual life goals. You may have a clear idea of what you want but you have little chance of success if your desires are not shared by your spouse. Your objectives during this phase should include the following:

• Involve your spouse in planning and decision making.

• Reach consensus on future goals.

• Identify relationship problems you want to correct.

• Focus on in-home adaptation.

***Organize Your Planning Materials:*** You may already have workspace for handling personal business, but it will probably be insufficient to handle the added materials involved in planning your retirement.

You will need a file cabinet and file folders. Set up files of magazine articles, newspaper clippings and correspondence about subjects of interest, activities, places to live, types of housing, etc. Develop a filing and storage system that keeps this data readily available. Your materials will not be of help if everything is piled in a box where it is difficult to reach. Go through your materials from time to time to see what other ideas are sparked. Also, make sure you are taking some action on things you are collecting, rather than simply filling file folders.

Set up an address file of organizations or other groups that are involved in things that interest you. This might be a 3" × 5" card file, spiral notebook or an address book.

Dedicate a calendar to retirement planning. You can use any convenient form, but record dates to attend meetings or take other actions associated with your preparation for retirement.

If you work in an office, consider setting up a second office at home. This will help compensate for the eventual loss of your office space at work and will facilitate your transition. Also, consider having personal stationery printed. This will help you maintain a sense of identity.

***Select Your Advisors:*** As you solidify your future plans you will need expert help. Develop a team of advisors you can turn to for legal, financial, tax, medical, insurance, real estate, estate planning and emotional advice. Solicit help from experts on the hobby, leisure and other activities you are interested in pursuing. If you plan to travel, get to know your travel agent.

Selecting expert advisors can be a challenge. Start by asking trusted friends for recommendations. Then, interview prospective advisors. During this process, find out at least three things:

- What are their professional credentials?

- Do they handle individuals with similar interests to yours?

- Are you comfortable with the person?

***Develop Other Interests:*** Acceptance is the time to start developing post-career plans. Leisure and other activities will take on major importance in retirement. Keep these two facts in mind:

- Rewarding interests and rich social ties can provide the fulfillment currently derived from work.

- Unrealistic expectations about the depth of your interests or strength of current social ties can leave you feeling betrayed, empty, depressed and without direction.

Fully evaluating your non-work activities and interests *before* retirement will help you avoid any unpleasant surprises. Part III of this book presents six chapters of alternative activities for you to consider.

It is not the quantity of outside interests you have that counts, it is the *quality.* A long list says little in itself. Test your hobbies and social plans to see if they are as rewarding as you imagine. Look for ways to become more deeply involved. Would lessons be appropriate? How about joining a club or participating in a show or tournament? Getting deeply involved with an activity will give you a clear picture of what role that activity can play in your future. If your interest turns out to be casual rather than all-consuming, you will know that other activities will be required to fill out your life in retirement.

If you do not have any current non-work interests, now is the time to seek out and try those that appeal to you. Begin by drawing up a list under the following headings:

> - Leisure Activities
>
> - Hobbies
>
> - Social Activities
>
> - Civic Organizations
>
> - Volunteer Organizations
>
> - Political Organizations

Take your time and sample the activities you have listed. Do not rush. It is not unreasonable for this to take a couple of years. When you finish, you will probably have found some activities you find very stimulating, some you are mildly interested in, and some that bore you. Then you can proceed to further developing those interests you find stimulating and worthwhile.

It is possible that you will find nothing that compares to the way work excites you. There is no sense in doing something just to keep busy. A day filled with meaningless activity is nothing to look forward to. If nothing beyond work holds any interest for you, explore the options of part-time work, going into business, or consulting, described in the next chapter.

***Resolve Housing Questions:*** In 1990, eighty-six percent of older Americans said they wanted to stay in their present home. This is not to say that you should not consider a move. However, relocating can be either a great adventure or a big mistake, depending upon how carefully you assess your needs and plan to meet them. The questionnaire, "Should I Move? Should I Stay?" will help focus your thinking:

## SHOULD I MOVE? SHOULD I STAY?

| Stay | Go |
|---|---|
| ____ 1. Taxes are lower where I am. | ____ I want to move where taxes are lower. |
| ____ 2. Prices are lower where I am. | ____ I want to move where prices are lower. |
| ____ 3. I want to live in a big city, enjoy cultural advantages. | ____ I want to live in a smaller town, enjoy small-town advantages. |
| ____ 4. I want to be with people of all ages. | ____ I want to be with people my own age. |
| ____ 5. I enjoy doing what I want when I want—I can do that right here. | ____ I want to move to a community where activities are planned. |
| ____ 6. I live in a good, safe neighborhood. | ____ My neighborhood is unsafe and becoming rundown. |
| ____ 7. I love the climate where I live now. | ____ I want to move to a different climate. |
| ____ 8. I want to be in familiar surroundings. | ____ I want something new and different. |
| ____ 9. I am doing all the things I enjoy doing right here. | ____ I want to go where I can enjoy new activities. |
| ____ 10. My children and grandkids live here and I want to be near them. | ____ Above all, I want a life separate from my kids. |
| ____ 11. I have friends here; I like it that way. | ____ I am ready to move away and make new friends. |
| ____ 12. I don't want to move away from my family doctors. | ____ I want to move to a place that has better health and medical facilities. |
| ____ 13. I have opportunities for part-time work here. | ____ I'd like to move where I might have more part-time opportunities. |
| ____ 14. I love my home, I want to stay and enjoy it. | ____ I am ready to move from my home and find a place easier to care for. |
| _____ Total | _____ Total |

If you are contemplating a move to another locality, use your vacation time to visit the area. As part of your assessment, be sure to visit the new location during its least desirable time of year. For example, visit Southern states such as Arizona or Florida in the summer and Northern and New England states in the winter.

The following points should help you come to a conclusion about whether to stay in your present home, move to a new home or apartment, retire to your vacation or second home, or move to a retirement community:

- *Proximity to activities:* Does the place you are considering have the kinds of activities you and your family are interested in pursuing?

- *Proximity to family and friends:* How important are family and friends in your daily life? It takes time to establish new friendships when you move.

- *Maintenance and upkeep:* Do you enjoy yard work and home maintenance? Does your present home require a lot of maintenance? Would you be better off in a smaller home, townhouse, condo or apartment?

- *Space requirements:* Is your present home too large? Is there space for each person to have a private retreat area—an office, workshop, studio, etc.?

- *Climate and geography:* With retirement, you have the freedom to choose your ideal location. Generally, climates with little fluctuation in temperature and little severe weather are favored.

- *Availability of Services:* Are medical, transportation and shopping facilities readily available? Many retirement communities are in picturesque but remote settings.

- *Quality of life:* There are quality-of-life tradeoffs among large cities, small towns, and rural areas. Consider such things as traffic, crime and congestion versus museums, theaters, shopping and services.

- *Cost of living:* Housing and other costs vary in different locations. Give consideration to initial cost of housing, resale possibilities, taxes—including property, income and sales taxes—and the costs of basic goods and services. In retirement communities, look specifically at assessments for services you may not utilize.

- *Safety features:* More than 22,000 people are killed each year in home accidents and more than 3 million become permanently disabled. Whether you stay or move, own or rent, be sure your home is safe for you and other occupants.

Building your retirement home, remodeling your present home, or simply redecorating your present home can help bring the reality of retirement into your life. Also, it can create potential problems between you and your spouse, unless the needs and desires of both are carefully considered and accommodated. This can be a real test of your consensus decision-making skills.

## Disengagement

At work, Disengagement signals the start of reducing your emotional and physical involvement in workplace activities. At home, it signals an increase in non-career activities. During this phase you take a more active role in integrating yourself into your non-career life. You need to finalize your retirement plans and put them into action.

***Foster a Positive Approach:*** Many people are reluctant to talk about retirement. But talking about your plans in a positive way can be tremendously beneficial. Home is the ideal place to put this notion into practice. Here, you can feel free to talk about retirement without worrying about your comments being misinterpreted or used inappropriately, which is often true at work. With retirement approaching, make a point of bringing it up in a positive context. The benefits you will receive include:

- Others can be a sounding board for your ideas.

- Others who have experience or knowledge that you do not have can contribute helpful comments.

- As you discuss retirement, you will be forced to become aware of your feelings.

- You will overcome any tendency to view retirement negatively.

- You will build momentum to get your plans under way.

- Through these conversations, you will increase your interest and involvement in others.

Each mention of retirement does not have to be a deep discussion of your plans, feelings and concerns. It can be a simple, casual but true, comment. For example, if someone asks about your plans this evening and you are attending a retirement planning seminar, say so. This may lead to further conversation, or the topic may be dropped.

***Review Your Plans:*** As with business plans, your post-career plans should be reviewed periodically. Here are some questions that will help you during the review:

• Are our goals still the same?

• What has happened since our last review that we should take into account?

• If our goals are still the same, what progress have we made?

• If we have not made much progress, what is the problem and what can we do about it?

• If our goals need to be modified, why and how?

A real test of your preparation is to project yourself a year or two into retirement, when you have settled into your planned post-career lifestyle. Take a typical month and lay out a loose schedule for every day of the month; use a monthly planning calendar and identify what you will be doing in the morning, afternoon and evening. You probably will not complete the schedule in one setting; work at blocking in a general agenda for each day. Now, how does it look? Are there gaps of time where you cannot figure out what to do? Do you really think you will want to play golf five days a week? Will one afternoon a week be sufficient to handle correspondence?

The goal of this exercise is not to develop a monthly schedule. It is to help you realize there are a lot of hours in a day, and many days in a month. If you cannot find something to do with them, they are worse than wasted. The by-product is boredom and depression. On the other hand, if you can fill the month with involving activities and projects, you will have a wealth of interests to draw on, every month of the year. Modify your plans as necessary to see that you are pursuing interests that provide you a rewarding retirement.

***Spreading the Word:*** As your retirement date approaches, send out announcements to your friends and relatives. A few simple words on how you want to share this happy occasion with them will suffice. If you have future plans you care to share, this is an excellent time to do so. You will probably receive a few retirement greeting cards in reply.

*Your Retirement Party:* The retirement event at work is a good-bye, so it is naturally infused with an undercurrent of sadness. For an uplifting experience, plan a retirement party at home; here, the underlying message is "hello," not "good-bye." The guest list should reflect where you are going with your life. For example:

- Neighbors you want to get to know

- Business associates with whom you would like to develop stronger ties

- Members of community groups with whom you plan to spend time

- Other retired people

- Friends to whom you hope to grow closer

Avoid inviting co-workers or colleagues who you probably will not be seeing much in the future.

## Redefinition

The Redefinition Phase begins when you leave work. When you have completed it, you will have successfully made your transition into retirement. This is the time when you put into operation all the plans you have been making.

The Redefinition Phase usually consists of three periods—celebration, transformation and settling in. It is not uncommon to take up to two years to complete this phase; seldom is it completed in less than six months.

*Celebration:* Immediately upon leaving work, many people embark upon a long anticipated vacation. Depending upon your preferences, this might be a cruise, foreign travel or travel within the U.S. A vacation at this time places you in familiar circumstances for not going to work. When the vacation is over, you will be ready to move forward with your plans and have little concern about not returning to the workplace.

*Transformation:* This is the period when you implement the changes in your life that come with your retirement. During this period, you will make any housing changes you plan to make. It is the time when you will become emersed in the activities you have chosen. It is also the time when you will incorporate changes in your daily routine that result from your retirement.

Many retirees look forward to changing such basic things, such as the hour they arise in the morning, whether they receive a morning or evening edition of the newspaper, and when they will handle household chores. Fill in the following schedule to reflect your preference of a typical day:

| | |
|---|---|
| M O R N I N G | |
| A F T E R N O O N | |
| E V E N I N G | |

Other routine items to be worked out include banking arrangements (i.e., was your bank convenient to your workplace, but inconvenient to your home?), the best time of day to go to the post office, and the most convenient place to get copies made. As you get involved in retirement, you will probably discover other things that need to be changed for your convenience.

***Settling In:*** This is truly an exciting time. There is a certain glamour associated with Celebration, and there is excitement in changes that comprise the Transformation. With these things behind you, you can begin to enjoy the rewards of your planning and preparation. Settling In is characterized by being comfortable with your new identity. You are actively involved in interests that have meaning for you, you have worked out a comfortable routine, and you and your spouse have worked out a sharing of household chores, as well as time together and time alone. This is where it was all headed. This is what retirement today is about.

## CONCLUSION

Transition at home is as equally important as transition at work. Other family members, particularly your spouse, must also make the transition. The transition can only be successful through working together.

Your spouse must move through the four phases of retirement alongside you. He or she must acknowledge that your retirement is an option in your lives and emotionally accept this as an option. Your spouse may see your retirement as a threat to his or her lifestyle, in terms of family income, freedom and status. These matters must be faced openly and resolved.

Your home will become the center for your retirement planning. Organize your space and materials to handle this new activity. Discuss plans, concerns and fears with family members. Include your spouse in decision making and planning that affects both of you. Be communicative and flexible as you pursue consensus on key issues.

Disengagement brings you opportunities to increase your family involvement as you decrease your work involvement. This can be a period of renewal in family relationships. Plan an appropriate announcement of your retirement to friends and relatives. Host a party for those who will be a part of your new lifestyle.

Approach Redefinition with flexibility. Seldom do things happen as smoothly as planned. If you have prepared well, you will be in a position to take advantage of the opportunities open to you. Your work is not finished; retirement is only a new beginning. It is up to you to keep it moving in the direction you want it to go. When you have objectives and plans for achieving them, you are halfway to your goal.

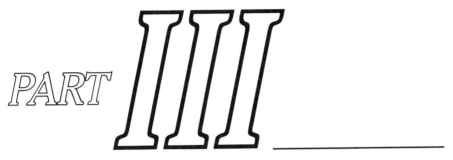

# PART III

# Choices for an Active Retirement

_____

# Chapter 6

# *Income Producing Activities*

---

Don Taylor just signed a four-year contract with the U.S. Postal Service that will keep him on his appointed rounds in the Lusk, WY area until he's 99. Six days a week he starts the day with 15 push-ups, 15 deep knee bends, and 600 steps on a treadmill. He then loads the mail into his pickup and drives 66.9 miles along dirt roads to deliver the mail to 29 ranching families.

Taylor started delivering mail in 1943 as a temporary when the regular postman went to war. He's been on the job ever since.

*USA Weekend*, September 8, 1991

---

Many of today's retirees want to stay active and involved in work for financial reasons, emotional reasons, or both. Here are a few facts about working after retirement:

- Nearly 25 percent of retirees hold jobs—about half for financial reasons and the other half for emotional reasons.

- About a third of the AARP's membership works, either full or part-time. Another third say they would like to be working.

• According to a study by Drake Beam Moran, Inc. of over 4,000 retiring executives, 49 percent became consultants or worked part-time, 13 percent took full-time jobs, and 12 percent went into business for themselves.

The bottom line is that some people should not retire to a life of non-work activities. You may be one of them. If so, you should view retirement as a time to work on your own terms rather than to stop working. This might mean doing something you have always wanted to do, such as starting your own business or teaching school. It might mean working on your own schedule as a part-time employee or consultant. Or, it might mean moving to the region of your choice and finding suitable full or part-time work there.

---

**Working in Retirement**

1. Are you considering any of the following income-producing activities in retirement?

  _____ Full-time employment

  _____ Part-time employment

  _____ Consulting

  _____ Going into your own business

2. If you are, what are your reasons?

  _____ I need the money

  _____ To be involved with people

  _____ To add meaning to my day

  _____ To achieve something worthwhile

  _____ To be part of an organization

---

In this chapter, four income producing activities will be explored—full-time employment, part-time employment, consulting and going into your own business.

## FULL-TIME EMPLOYMENT

Begin your quest for new employment with a careful analysis of what you have to offer a prospective employer and an analysis of what you consider the ideal position. The task throughout your job search will be to find where these two come together.

Few people are aware of the many career opportunities that match their individual skills and interests. Look for activities within careers that use your favored skills, and the problems your skills can solve. Where would you like to work? What kind of organization appeals to you? What kind of work environment do you prefer? Do you prefer to work alone or with others? These are the kinds of questions you need to answer as you match your skills and interests to an employment opportunity. Finally, do not get caught up with status. If you are interested in keeping busy, making new friends and staying in contact with the public, a lower-level job might be right for you. Also, they are usually easier to find.

Include a visit to your local library within your analysis. Here, two books published by the United States Department of Labor will be particularly helpful in directing you to career opportunities. *The Occupational Outlook Handbook* is updated every two years and describes over 200 occupations, what the jobs consist of, where they are performed, salaries, and education and training requirements. This handbook also directs you to additional sources of information about occupations.

*The Dictionary of Occupational Titles* contains more than 17,500 classified and described occupations, each with a unique occupational code and title. The classification system helps identify skills that are transferable within industries and among related technologies. Titles are arranged by occupational groups, industry and alphabetically.

Your purpose here is to broaden the array of opportunities that might interest you, opportunities you might never consider without investigation. Perusing opportunities that match your peculiar mix of skills and interests might present you with your ideal career opportunity. After you narrow the possibilities, interview people in your fields of interest. This does two things: It confirms that the career matches your interests, and it establishes valuable contacts.

You *can* get a job during retirement. It may not be easy, but it is not impossible. Because the demographic shift in the labor market is making fewer and fewer younger workers available, many companies are hiring older workers. Your key to success will be presenting yourself so that your skills are noticed more than your age.

## Attitude

If you think you are too old, you will not get the job. You will communicate your attitude, which will be your downfall. Recognize that most of the negatives you feel about your age are based upon misconceptions about older workers. In reality, older workers have more going for them than against them. When preparing for your job search, keep these very real assets in mind—assets that many employers are finding more and more attractive:

- *Expertise:* Your expertise, gained from years of experience, far outweighs what younger candidates can offer. As many recruiters are beginning to realize, an academic background is not equivalent to on-the-job experience. Plus, you will not be concerned about promotions, and you can be a mentor to less experienced staff.

- *Dependability:* You can be counted on. Older workers are more dependable than their younger colleagues. Statisitcs show they have better attendance records—they take fewer sick days and are more punctual.

- *Stability:* Older workers are less inclined than younger workers to leave the company. For example, Days Inn reports that it loses about 40 percent of its reservation agents each year. The turnover rate for *older* agents is only 1 percent.

So, being past a certain age does not mean you are too old. It does mean, however, that you are experienced, dependable and stable. In other words, you are a great job candidate.

## Preparing Your Resume

Not everyone will need a resume. You may be able to get the job you want through personal contacts. However, if you do need a resume, you will want one that works for you, not against you.

Modern resumes are no longer a dull listing of past jobs. They are directed specifically to the job being sought; they are positive, functional descriptions of skills, qualifications and achievements important to that position. An effective resume advertises you honestly to prospective employers. Jobs go to those who sell themselves most effectively. Many resume writers fail to understand that selling yourself is what is important.

Age-proof your resume—remove anything that emphasizes your age. Dates draw attention to your age; you want to emphasize skills and accomplishments. Do this by playing down or omitting dates, including when you attended school, were in the military, and held various jobs. Do not include your earliest jobs. They emphasize the number of years you have been working, yet have little bearing today on your marketable skills. If you list activities you are involved in, leave out any that would identify you as a senior citizen.

Be specific in your descriptions of what you have accomplished. Avoid vague generalizations and pat phrases. Being older means you have expertise on your side. Let it come through in your resume. Cite concrete examples of specific accomplishments. For example, "managed a department of five staff with an annual budget of $850,000." Avoid superlatives. Look for quantifiable activities that saved or made your employer money, such as increased production, improved operations, or improved work environment.

Resumes with eye appeal capture the attention of prospective readers. This requires proper grammar, spelling, punctuation and accurate typing. Keep your resume short. You do not want to tell everything in the resume—save something for the interview. If possible, limit yourself to one 8-1/2 by 11 inch page. If you need more space, put essential data on the first page, and use a second page for backup data. The following resume guidelines will help you paint a positive picture of yourself:

- Use short paragraphs with double-spacing between.

- Leave wide margins.

- Use captial letters or boldface type for headings and descriptive titles.

- Type titles either flush with left margin or centered.

- Use bullets, stars or underscores for emphasis.

- Use the full page, distributing white space between sections.

- Use simple language and no acronyms.

Two resume formats are generally used. One is chronological, the other is functional. The functional format is usually superior for the older worker. It presents skills and accomplishments in the order of their importance, rather than in the order they were acquired. You can emphasize skills acquired through experiences other than in the workplace. A well prepared resume includes the following categories of information:

- *Objective:* Your job objective statement is the single most important statement in your resume. You cannot write an effective resume until you clearly define and state your job objective. An effective job objective statement presents your objective. It also highlights your skills and attributes that are of greatest benefit to your prospective employer. For example: "An appointment to faculty position where classroom instructional skills and knowledge of management theory can be combined to train future business leaders."

- *Experience:* The experience you include should support your stated objective. Do not include anything that is not germane. If possible, categorize your experience under appropriate skill headings and list your achievements under each category. An applicant for a faculty position, for example, might list Curriculum Design, Instructional Methodology and Evaluation Techniques as skills headings, with achievements listed beneath each.

- *Work History:* List each position you have held during the last 15 to 20 years. Indicate periods of employment by years, for example, 1983–1992. If you held several positions in the same field with one employer, consolidate the jobs and focus on the more recent work.

- *Education:* If appropriate to the position you seek, list your education, starting with your highest college degree. Show the name of the institution, the state where you attended school, and any awards or recognition you received. Include other relevant courses you have completed, such as apprenticeships, military training and self-help courses.

- *Other Facts:* Choose something distinguishing and appropriate to the position and prospective employer for the reader to remember about you. List it under a specific heading such as publications, professional affiliations, licenses or hobbies. Do not include personal information, references or salary history, which can be developed, as appropriate, after the interview.

## Sample Resume

**Marion E. Haynes**

5223 Imogene Street                                  (713) 668-3273
Houston, TX 77096-2515

**Job Objective**

Faculty appointment as adjunct associate professor where classroom instructional skills and knowledge of management theory can be used to train future business leaders.

**Experience**

*Curriculum Design*

- Served as staff associate to training manager, designing training programs and materials for presentation by staff instructors.
- Designed own curriculum for classroom presentation at two major universities.
- Have designed educational experiences to teach managers and supervisors such diverse skills as interpersonal communications, public speaking, leadership, how to conduct effective meetings, and how to manage by objectives.

*Instructional Methodology*

- Experienced lecturer—past president of local Toastmasters Club.
- Adept at using experiential and laboratory techniques such as role play, unstructured groups and structured group experiences.

*Evaluation Techniques*

- Well grounded in evaluation techniques from participant evaluations to behavioral change research.

**Education**

New York University, MBA (with distinction)
Arizona State University, BS, Business Administration


**Experience**

- Shell Oil Company
  Management and Organization development—17 years
- University of Houston
  Workshop Instructor—4 years
- Houston Baptist University
  Adjunct Instructor—3 years

**Publications**

- 25 articles and 8 book reviews in various trade and professional journals
- 6 books with some translated into Arabic, French and German

## Developing Leads

A Department of Labor study noted that employees of all ages found jobs in these ways: 48 percent through personal leads from friends, relatives and colleagues; 24 percent through direct contact with employers; 6 percent from school placement centers; 5 percent from help wanted ads; 3 percent from state employment offices; and 13 percent from a variety of other leads.

The majority of people over fifty find jobs by networking. Generally, it is a waste of time and money to mail resumes in response to newspaper ads. You should avoid using your resume unless it is necessary. Here are some ideas on developing leads:

*Talk to friends and colleagues.* Personal referrals are still the best way to land a job. Talk to anyone and everyone—friends and acquaintances, relatives, people you do business with—you never know who knows whom. When you talk with people, tell them you are looking for a job. Be specific about what you are looking for. People cannot help you if you do not give them enough information.

*Maintain your memberships in professional associations.* This will keep you up-to-date on what is happening in your profession. In addition to talking with people you know, listen to conversations around you. You might overhear something useful.

*Draw on your contacts in organizations.* Hobby clubs, health clubs, church organizations, night school classes and community organizations are good places to hear about job leads. Let your fellow members know of your interests.

*Consider joining a self-help group.* Being around others in similar circumstances can provide support and motivation. For managers and professonals, membership in 40-Plus may be the best way back into the mainstream of your profession. 40-Plus is a private, non-profit organization, with sixteen clubs in major cities. You must be forty years or older to join, and have an average income of $30,000 or more during the previous three years. AARP's Works program offers a series of job-hunting and career development workshops in thirteen cities across the country. The Senior Career Planning and Placement Service specializes in finding jobs for retired executives. You can contact them at

257 Park Avenue South, New York, NY 10010. These and other, similar organizations can be a tremendous help to you.

***Use the services of Operation ABLE.*** Operation ABLE provides assistance to older job hunters in Arkansas, California, Massachusetts, Michigan, Nebraska, New York and Vermont.

***Register with your state employment service.*** These offices provide a clearing house for matching applicants and jobs. They also offer job skills training, job-search workshops, and individual job counseling. They tend to be more effective for those seeking middle and lower level opportunities.

***Sign up with a private placement agency.*** Private agencies are more effective with middle and higher level positions. Many agencies specialize in a profession or type of employment and therefore may be more familiar with opportunities in their narrow segment of industry. Private agencies charge a fee for their services. Be sure you know the full terms of your commitment before signing a contract. Some employers pay agency fees, but you should not assume that your placement will be handled this way.

***Send out targeted sales letters.*** Use a letter, rather than a resume, when you contact a company directly. A well written letter can get you an interview. Include only the information that sells you. Outline the qualifications that make you right for a job at the company. List your specific accomplishments.

## Successful Interviewing

It may be a long time since you had a job interview. Many retirees have spent their entire career with the same company, so they have had little opportunity to practice successful interviewing skills.

Thre are two general types of placement interviews: the *screening* interview and the *selection* interview. In the screening interview, a member of the recruitng staff talks with a large number of applicants to find the most promising candidates. The interview focuses on work experience, education and training. They are used to identify candidates qualified enough to be considered further.

The selection interview determines who will get the job. It is conducted by the actual person who is hiring. You would want to impress this person with your accomplishments and your ability to work well with the work group.

You have three goals during an interview. First, you must determine if the available job is right for you. Ask questions to fully understand the nature and scope of the job. Second, if the job appears right, you must project the image that you are the person the company needs. Third, you may have the opportunity to have a job created to utilize your unique skills. It is not unusual for an interview to result in a different job offer than was originally sought.

Remember, the interview is make or break time. It is up to you to prove that you are right for the job. The real key is believing in yourself, which is the only way you can present yourself in the best possible way. Here are some key points that will produce success:

- *Keep faith in yourself.* Even if you have experienced a number of unsuccesful interviews, continue to think of yourself as a winner. Review the high points of your life. Read uplifting books. Listen to motivational tapes. Interviewing is salesmanship. Assertive, confident people sell best.

- *Make a good impression.* People make judgments on what you appear to be. Your first impression is far more important than your credentials. The first five minutes sets the tone for the rest of the interview. Be sure to look and act like a successful, polished professional. Pay special attention to your appearance and remember the little things like polished shoes, trimmed hair, and well groomed hands and nails. When you walk in, shake hands firmly, smile pleasantly and maintain an upright posture. Speak in a voice that is strong, but not overbearing.

- *Do not apologize.* Older workers frequently apologize for their age. This is a mistake. Instead, start out positively. Emphasize the advantages of hiring someone with your level of expertise.

- *Emphasize specific accomplishments.* Your experience is the greatest thing you have going for you. Bring up your accomplishments during the interview. Study a list of your achievements and be prepared to present detailed information on each.

- *Do not overdo it.* The real skill of selling is to know when you have made the sale and close on it. All too often, sales are lost from overselling, rather than underselling. Do not dominate the interview or you may come across as overbearing. Present just enough information to close the deal.

- *Delay giving your resume.* Hold off as long as you can. Sell the interviewer through conversation. Explain that you have the right background, the right combination of expertise for the job. After you have sold him or her, hand over your resume.

Most of your preparation for the interview should focus on your own qualifications and on learning something about the company. Different interviewers have different styles and use different techniques to find out about applicants. These questions are commonly asked by interviewers:

- *Tell me about yourself.* This is an opportunity for you to talk about your skills and accomplishments, relevant to the position. Do not mention achievements or skills that might show you to be overly qualified and do not get into personal characteristics or insights that are not appropriate for the opening.

- *Why do you want to work here?* Emphasize what you can do for them, rather than just what you hope to gain.

- *What is your greatest strength?* Use this question as an opportunity to showcase your skills, backed up with accomplishments that provide credibility.

- *What is your greatest weakness?* Strengths used to extremes become weaknesses. Point out that you may occasionally overdo something. Or, try to find a perceived weakness that is, in fact a strength for the position.

- *What did you like most and least about past jobs?* Here again, be selective. Mention things you liked most that are relevant to the present opening and things you liked least that are unimportant to the present job.

- *What makes you qualified for this position?* Here is another opportunity to highlight your skills and your accomplishments that are important to the job you are seeking.

- *Why are you interested in a job below your qualifications?* Explain that your interests have changed. You no longer want the stress of your prior position. Also, money is no longer your primary concern.

Point out your transferable skills that you can use in a new career that provide a better balance for your current lifestyle.

Close the interview by asking for the position. Consider asking: "Do you think I can do the job?" This question can be answered only with a *yes* or a *no*. If the interviewer says no, ask: "Where do you think I don't measure up to your requirements?" The interviewer's response will open up an opportunity for you to clarify any skills or abilities that show your qualifications. If you are unqualified, it lets you know where you need to improve.

If the interviewer says yes to your question, ask: "Are you going to make me an offer?" If you do not get a definite answer immediately, ask for a specific date for a final decision. If you are interested in it, never end an interview without asking for the job.

---

**Characteristics that Help and Hinder Applicants***

| Help | Hinder |
|------|--------|
| • Good first impression | • Bad first impression |
| • Confidence | • Arrogance |
| • Enthusiasm | • Pushy attitude |
| • Sincerity | • Interrupting |
| • Honesty | • Talking too much |
| • Good communications skills | • Evasiveness |
| • Pleasing personality | • Lack of confidence |
| • Applicable job skills | • Lack of job skills |

* Based on a survey of 625 California business executives conducted in 1989 by Thomas Temporaries of Irvine, CA.

---

## Companies Open to Older Workers

With the number of teenagers shrinking, jobs that were traditionally filled by teenagers are being filled by older workers. This is particularly noticeable in the retail, restaurant and hotel industries.

Following is a sampling of companies with reputations for hiring older workers. If you are interested, contact the company's operations in your community. Opportunities will, of course, depend on available openings.

Aetna Life & Casualty
American Airlines
American Express
Connecticut General Life
   Insurance Company
Control Data Corporation
Corning Glass Works
Days Inn of America, Inc.
DuPont
Equitable Life Assurance
   Society
Exxon
Firestone Tire & Rubber Company
General Dynamics
General Electric
Hewlett-Packard
Honeywell
IBM
Kentucky Fried Chicken
Levi Strauss & Co.
Lockheed Company
McDonald's Corp.
Merck & Company

Atlantic Richfield Company
Borg-Warner Corporations
Citicorp
Metropolitan Life Insurance
Morgan Guaranty Trust Co.
Motorola
Mutual of Omaha
Northrop Corp.
Northwest Mutual Life Ins.
Oscar Mayer
Pfizer
Polaroid Corp.
Shell Oil Company
Sherwin-Williams Co.
The Toro Company
Travelers Insurance
   Companies
Wells Fargo & Company
Wilson Foods
Woodward & Lothrop
   Department Stores
Wm. Wrigley Jr. Co.
Xerox Corporation

## Consider Nonprofit Organizations

Retirees with less concern about financial rewards can find some very satisfying employment opportunities with nonprofit organizations. The variety of opportunities is broad enough to accommodate just about any kind of experience you might have.

Approximately 1.3 million charities, church groups, foundations, schools, agricultural co-ops, quasi-governmental bodies plus arts, health, social-service, and educational organizations operate on a nonprofit basis. They employ more than 20 million people and generate annual revenues of $750 billion. You can get a nonprofit organization listing from your state commerce division or county clerk.

Tapping into the realm of nonprofits is as simple as deciding what cause you are motivated to support. Do you want to eliminate world hunger, provide homes for low income families, help stamp out illiteracy, protect the environment, or feed the homeless? There is a place for you and your talents wherever your heart leads you. Generally, work opportunities can be divided into two major categories— direct involvement in the organization's mission and indirect involvement or administrative support. Pick your cause and your involvement. Then, follow the job search instructions in this chapter to a truly fulfilling experience.

## PART-TIME EMPLOYMENT

Part-time employment allows time for other things such as travel and/or volunteer work. Thre are three types of part-time arrtangements to consider: *on-going part-time* work, the more traditional arrangement, involves working a few hours each day, or a few days each week, on a regular basis. *Intermittent* work is done on a full-time schedule for a period of time. This arrangement accommodates travel very nicely. *Job sharing*, common with small firms that have most flexibility in personnel policy administration, requires two or three workers to assume responsibility for one full-time job. Typically, those sharing the job are given the freedom to handle their own scheduling. They assure that the job is covered and keep the employer advised of who will be there. This can be an ideal arrangement for older workers, if they are *reliable* partners who can work out their schedules to accommodate individual interests.

Finding part-time work involves all the job search skills discussed under full-time employment. Keep in mind that you also have the opportunity to sell your potential employer on part-time employment. Sometimes the employer has not considered a part-time option; suggesting it can solve a problem for both of you.

The service industries, particularly the fast food industry, are most open to hiring older, part-time workers. Both McDonald's and Kentucky Fried

Chicken, where workers can set their own hours actively seek retirees for part-time work. Lodging and retail sales have similar opportunities.

## Retiree Job Banks

Several companies have job banks that match their own retirees interested in part-time work with opportunities within their organization. Travelers Insurance Companies in Hartford, Connecticut began such a program in 1981. Because of the demand for older, part-time workers, Travelers expanded its program in 1985, to recruit retirees of other insurance companies. Companies with similar programs include IBM, Atlantic Richfield Company, Wells Fargo Bank, and Aerospace Corporation of Southern California. Your previous employer is an obvious starting place in your search for part-time work.

## Government Subsidized Employment

If you are near the poverty line, you may qualify for part-time federal public service work. The Senior Community Service Employment Program (SCSEP) provides part-time employment for low-income unemployed seniors. To be eligible you must be 55 years or older, have an income of no more than 125 percent of the poverty level, and be unemployed.

This program is administered by the U.S. Department of Labor through national organizations and state agencies.

The work provided is at minimum wage and averages 20 to 25 hours a week. The jobs are public service in educational and social service agencies such as elderly nutrition centers. Inquire at your local Agency on Aging.

## Temporary Help Agencies

Retirees represent the fastest growing segment of temporary help services. The Bureau of Labor Statistics reports that 98 percent of U.S. companies use temporary workers. In 1988, there were 1,000,000 temporary workers; 9.7 percent were 55 years and older. The distribution of jobs in 1990 was:

- 63.5 percent office and clerical
- 15.4 percent industrial workers
- 11.2 percent technical and professional
- 9.9 percent medical

The temporary help industry seeks retired workers because many of their customers prefer them. Older workers know the job, have an excellent work ethic, are responsible, and have good attendance records.

Temproary work can be ideal for retirees. It offers a way to get out into the world, doing something worthwhile, developing new friends and supplementing retirement income. Temporary employment offers flexibility on scheduling. You can work several days, several weeks, or a month or two at a time. By registering with several agencies, you can decide when and where you will work.

In 1988, Kelly Services began its Encore Program, to recruit workers over age 55. The program provides training in computers, research and office management. Other temporary agencies include Accountemps, a subsidiary of Robert Half International that specializes in financial professionals and executives: Lawsmiths, which began in 1985 as a temporary service for lawyers; and Locum Tenens, with offices in Atlanta and Denver, which began placing doctors in temporary assignments in 1983. These agencies illustrate the diversity of opportunities for temporaries. The yellow pages of your local phone book will include agencies serving your community.

Becoming associated with an agency is much like the employment process. You will be interviewed, and perhaps tested, for job skills. They will conduct a background investigation to verify your credentials and experience. If you meet the agency's qualification requirements, you will be placed in a pool of workers seeking similar work. When a client requests help, the agency will select workers from the pool of registered applicants. The agency's goal is to meet its clients' requirements to continue getting those clients' business.

Benefits vary from agency to agency. All must meet federal and state requirements for workers' compensation, unemployment compensation and Social Security. Some provide a minimum of other benefits. A few give a full range of benefits, including vacations, paid holidays, insurance, profit sharing, merit pay increases, and bonuses.

## CONSULTING

A consultant provides technical or professional custom services to a client for a fee. As a consultant, you are free to work as much or as little as you wish. This makes consulting very appealing to retirees.

Consulting is a lot like temporary work. You work on a per-project basis, removed from the daily stress of a regular job. Meanwhile, you are able to use your skills.

Many consultants get started by working for their former employer. They then expand their practice by adding other companies in their field—often, companies that are suppliers or clients of their former employer. This is a logical extension of their background and a great way to use their experience.

Companies use consultants to help meet deadlines, provide skills the company lacks, cover understaffing, provide an objective third-party viewpoint from outside the company, and handle sensitive or politically charged situations that are best done by an outsider.

If you are seriously considering consulting, make sure your capabilities are compatible with the requirements of the job. In addition to technical or professional skills, you need to be comfortable approaching people and selling yourself and your ideas. Not everyone is cut out to be a consultant. It requires a motivated self-starter who is comfortable working alone.

### Getting Started

The first issue to decide is the scope of your practice. Will you operate locally, within a region, nationally or internationally? How large do you expect your business to become? Will you be a one-person operation or add others to your staff? In many cases, it is best to remain a one-person practice. Will you offer products as well as services?

Most consultants open their first offices in their homes—it keeps the costs down. Also, location generally is not important as you will contact clients by phone or letter and visit them at their place of business. You have three choices if a home-based operation is not practical for you—a convenience office, a shared office, or a private office.

A convenience office is working space within a complex of other offices that share common support services. Each office is separate but shares the reception area, typing, copying, phone answering, conference rooms and other office amenities. Some even offer accounting and billing services.

Shared office space involves joining up with another consultant. If you carefully select who you share space with, you can also gain through the contacts and business referrals you receive, as well as the sharing of office overhead expenses.

A private office is the most expensive option. However, you are in control. You do not have to negotiate with others for the services you need. You can save money by using an answering machine and arranging part-time typing, copying and bookkeeping services.

If your consulting work is regulated by state standards, you may need to obtain a professional license. Accountants, engineers and health services are among those requiring such licenses. Check with your state's department of Consumer Affairs. You also may need a business license. These are generally issued by the city or county where your office is located. Check with your city clerk's office.

If you sell products, you may need a sales tax permit, which allows you to collect sales tax and transmit it to the state. It also permits you to avoid sales tax on things you buy for resale and lets you buy supplies at wholesale prices. Check with your state's tax board.

If you name your business something other than your own name, you will need to file with your county clerk to use a fictitious name. This establishes the relationship between you and your practice as a matter of public record.

Howard L. Shenson, a certified management consultant, is a leader in the consulting industry. He specializes in marketing professional practices and information services on seminars, newsletters and consulting. If you are serious about consulting, you may wish to contact him about his educational packages. His address is 20750 Ventura Blvd., Woodland Hills, CA 91364; telephone (808) 703-1415.

## Pricing Your Services

Consultants charge for their services in several ways. The most common are an hourly or daily rate, per project, and by retainer. Charging a fixed price per project is generally preferred by clients and can be the most profitable to you.

What you can charge will depend upon your expertise, personal reputation, record of achievements, credentials, marketing effectiveness, competition, and value to the client. To be profitable, your fee schedule must consider three major areas:

- *Salary:* Set a base salary for yourself, consistent with what others doing similar work are paid.

- *Overhead:* This includes all the direct and indirect costs of doing business. Expenses are either client-related, which are charged to the client in addition to your fee, or general expenses which are charged to overhead. General expenses include rent, telephone, licenses and permits, and advertising.

- *Profit:* Your fee should include a profit margin above the cost of salary and overhead. Profit and salary are not the same. You are entitled to both and should factor them into your fee.

Discovering the fee range for the type of consulting service you offer enables you to decide intelligently where to price your services, based on your salary, overhead and profit expectations in relation to competition. Ultimately, the value of your service will be determined by what your clients are willing to pay. It is your job to convince them you are the best at any price.

## Marketing Your Services

A public relations firm can provide professional guidance in marketing your services. The starting place is usually to design stationery, business cards, and a descriptive brochure that present a professional image. These will be the first contact potential clients have with you, and they need to make a good impression. With these tools in hand, you pursue three main marketing strategies of networking, publicity, and advertising:

*Networking:* Networking will probably be your most productive marketing strategy. Through contacts with career colleagues and friends, you begin by building a reputation and business with your prior employer; you grow by expanding to other companies within the industry.

Your network should include membership in at least two associations—a trade or professional association and a consultant's association. Getting involved in associations gets you valuable exposure from rubbing shoulders with those who are in a position to help you the most. Consider joining a community or business group such as the Lions Club, Chamber of Commerce, and Women in Business.

*Publicity:* Free publicity of newspaper, radio and television interviews is the best kind of promotion. It lends credibility and gets your name before the public. Writing articles for magazines and newspapers is another way to get free publicity and advance your image as an expert. This can be especially productive when you write for professional or trade magazines that are read by your potential clients. Making speeches and conducting seminars also bring in prospects and expand your network.

*Advertising:* A telephone book yellow pages listing is very effective for most businesses. One basic entry is included in the cost for your business phone. Enhancements are extra.

Beyond this, newspaper advertising can be a low cost way of reaching a large number of people. Trade and professional magazine advertising can pinpoint your audience. Direct mailing is expensive and draws low response rates; however, with a carefully developed mailing list, it can pay off.

## Dealing with Clients

In many situations, a number of people will be involved in the decision to hire you. Therefore, it is important to identify the role each person will play in the decision and who you, in fact, will be working for, if you are hired. Three categories of roles frequently exist:

- *Initiator:* The one who contacts you with a problem to solve

- *Permitter:* The one who agrees to contract for your services

- *Authorizer:* The one with authority to spend the organization's money and must approve your contract

In discussions with those engaging your services, it is appropriate to ask, "Who else must agree to engage my services?" and "Who must authorize the project?"

**The Proposal:** After meetings with the prospective client, you should draw up and submit a written proposal. This should include:

- A statement of the situation or problem

- Objective of the project

- A description of the scope of the project—what *will* and *will not* be done

- A list of the tasks you will do

- Who will do the project and who will be the client contact

- Time estimated to complete the project with starting and targeted completion dates

- Your fee for the project, plus terms of payment—interim payments or upon completion

- Benefits the client can expect

**Progress Report:** Before you begin the project, give your client a project plan showing the steps involved in completing the project and the schedule for each step. Then provide written progress reports against this plan, summarizing progress made on each task; list any obstacles that are causing problems. Besides being excellent records of your progress, as the project is carried out these reports reduce the chances of misunderstanding and changes in project scope.

**Final Report:** Each project should be wrapped up with a written report that summarizes your findings and recommendations. The report should indicate areas that need additional work and changes that should be considered beyond the scope of the project.

*Follow-Up:* The most important phase of a project is follow-up telephone calls. These calls give you an opportunity to monitor reactions to changes initiated by your client, and often lead to subsequent assignments. If progress is not being made, you may be able to provide the encouragement needed to move the implementation forward. Follow-up is the secret to good referrals, satisfied customers and a strong, consulting practice.

## OPERATING YOUR OWN BUSINESS

If you have dreamed of owning your own business, retirement can be the perfect opportunity to realize that dream. Your retirement income can provide a base of financial support to get you through the initial start-up and help you weather the inevitable ups and downs of a new venture. In addition to a financial base, you have both the time to invest and the experiences of a lifetime to draw upon.

The business world is a demanding, unforgiving place; being very good at what you do is important to your success. You have to be good to be a viable competitor. And, enjoying what you are doing to the point of doing it even if you do not have to, will help keep you going when times are rough.

Working for yourself requires you to be organized and a self-starter. It takes self-discipline to do what has to be done. It helps to set a schedule and stick to it, as though you were working for someone else.

Starting a business is a risk—and some people are not comfortable taking risks. (See the Risk Taking Quiz in Chapter 12.) According to the Small Business Administration, three out of four businesses fail in their first year of operation; nine out of ten fail within ten years.

If you have the entrepreneurial spirit, you will be willing to take this risk. Also, you will have the drive and persistence to keep going when things get tough. Failures will be seen as opportunities to learn how to do better next time. You will take charge of the situation and allow your creativity to overcome the obstacles. Above all, you will believe in yourself and your ability to succeed. (See pp. 91–92, *An Entrepreneur's Core Beliefs.*)

## An Entrepreneur's Core Beliefs

It is a person's beliefs which pave the way for success or dig the rut of mediocrity. Evaluate your beliefs against this list. Do you have the beliefs of an entrepreneur?

### 1. Security is an inside job.

It is false to assume that financial security comes from a job, a market or an industry. "Security" only comes from within. Entrepreneurs know that, "If it's going to be, it's up to me." Real security is internal and eternal.

### 2. I'll never get rich working at a JOB.

No one ever gets rich working at a job. Success belongs to those who take action toward financial success by stepping out of a job.

### 3. I can be rich.

Entrepreneurs believe they most certainly can and will become rich because they believe in striving for big goals and in their ultimate success.

### 4. It is by giving that we receive.

Entrepreneurs are always thinking of how they can give more service. In providing a quality product or service, entrepreneurs win and so do their clients.

### 5. The customer is king.

In business, the customer is king. Kings must be made happy, regardless of whether they are nasty or nice. Any entrepreneur whose interest or allegiance is not to the customer will soon fail.

### 6. Be driven by passion.

People of passion persevere. People who lack passion sacrifice quality for quantity, accept mediocrity, and are duly rewarded for their humble efforts.

### 7. I am responsible for my income.

Responsibility is believing that income has more to do with a mindset than markets, more to do with attitudes than recessions. Entrepreneurs make things happen regardless of what *everyone* else says.

**8. Change is good.**

Entrepreneurs know that adaptability is an essential part of winning. They seek to improve personal and company productivity and profits. They see change as a necessity for reaching their goals, and believe change is the natural process for improvement.

**9. Action.**

Planning is necessary, and life could not function without it. But entrpreneurs know that only unceasing and highly directed action leads to success.

**10. Risk is a virtue.**

In a world of caution, security and collateral, risk seems almost ludicrous. The forfeiting of comfortable lifestyles for the uncertainty of an entrepreneurial venture seems foolish, except to the entrepreneur who enjoys the freedom and the lifestyle of his choosing.

**11. Goals are absolutely essential.**

Few people ever succeed without defining and writing their goals. Goals keep entrepreneurs going and maintaining their focus through the fog of battle.

**12. Do it despite the fear.**

Most people think fear means stop, retreat, give up. To entrepreneurs, fear is just an emotion; it doesn't mean stop, go or otherwise. Often the difference between winning and losing is the amount of action they take when they are experiencing the discomfort of fear.

**13. Constant training is crucial.**

The winners in business know their real assets are their people. People and their development have to be a priority. Training and personal development are never expenses to the successful entrpreneur, they are investments in the future growth of their enterprise.

---

Developed by Bob Proctor, educator, business consultant, convention speaker, and entrepreneur. Used by permission.

To do well, take time to research your market and learn the ins and outs of operating a small business. You can avoid many of the pitfalls that lead others to failure by being well informed before you jump in.

## Choices Available

There are more than 13 million businesses in the United States. The Small Business Administration classifies 97 percent as small businesses; 79 percent of these are home-based. You can conveniently blend your part-time, home-based operation with your other retirement activities, or you can operate a full-fledged, fiercely competitive business. The choice is yours.

Many home-based businesses grow out of hobbies. Do you have a craft or skill that you could put to use producing marketable products? Other businesses grow out of special interests, such as operating a one vehicle limousine service. The range of choices is limited only by your imagination.

You can start a full-fledged operation from scratch, by buying an existing business, or by teaming up with a franchisor. Each has pluses and minuses. There can be more personal satisfaction by starting a business from scratch and growing it to a successful operation. Your risk of failure is increased because the business has no track record. There may not be enough market for another establishment or your product or service may not appeal to your potential clientele.

Before buying an existing business, you can analyze its past performance and get an idea of its potential for success. Be aware that you may have to overcome a negative image in the marketplace, and your initial investment may be greater, to compensate for the existing clientele. Franchise operations have a greater chance of success; they offer a proven business approach, marketplace appeal, training and counseling, and site selection expertise. You will pay for this backing with an initial investment plus a percentage of profits, and you will be required to follow specific business practices.

The most successful businesses fulfill special needs. Find a unique angle that gives your business an advantage; discover something different or a new twist to an old product or service. Think like a customer. Why would you, as a customer, want to buy your product or service, rather than patronize someone already in business? The answer may be your location, delivery, quality, hours of service, customer service, product choices, price or some other feature unique to your particular venture.

## Develop a Business Plan

Successful businesses start with well thought-out plans. Yet, surveys indicate that more than 50 percent of new business owners have never prepared a business plan. A business plan is a road map describing the assumptions that form the basis for your business and a timetable for implementing it. It helps you think through your problems on paper before you invest your money. The business plan is a starting plan that must be modified as experience is gained in operating the business. Just as you modify your travel plans when you encounter some obstacle, you will need to modify your business plan when something unexpected crops up. The following topics are essential elements to include in your business plan:

I. Competition
—Who are your competitors?
—What do they charge for their products or services?

II. Capital
—How much money do you have to invest?
—Where can you get additional capital?

III. Startup Costs
—Facilities
—Equipment and furniture
—Professional fees
—Office supplies
—Inventory
—Sales literature
—Phone installation
—Utilities deposits
—Working capital

IV. Expenses
—Rent
—Utilities
—Supplies

—Insurance
—Taxes
—Maintenance
—Advertising

V. Income

VI. Break-even Volume

As your business progresses, you will be able to monitor actual experience against your plan. It will alert you to potential problems in time to deal with them before disaster strikes. It will also verify the success you are experiencing, if that is the case, so you will be able to enjoy the satisfaction you have earned through careful planning and hard work.

## Sources of Help

The Small Business Administration has several ways to help you get started. A toll-free call to their answer desk [(800) 827-5722] will get you information on how to develop a business plan, where to get training and how to obtain financing, including Small Business Administration loans. They will send you a start-up kit containing a list of over fifty publications, planning guides and other helpful information.

Small Business Development Centers are located in every state, generally near colleges or universities. They offer management assistance, training and counseling. The Service Corps of Retired Executives (SCORE) provides counseling and free advice, as well as workshops on how to start a business. SCORE will be listed in your local phone book. Your local library can also tell you how to contact them.

## THE DOWNSIDE OF EARNING INCOME IN RETIREMENT

Our tax system does not encourage retirees to earn income. You need to look carefully at the net effect of your earnings, and plan your income to minimize any adverse effect. In addition to the graduated schedule of Federal Income Taxes, consider the effect of earnings on Social Security benefits and the cost of the Self-Employment Tax.

## Earnings and Social Security

Social Security has an Earnings Limitation that applies until you reach the age of 70. It works like this:

During the tax year of 1992 for ages 62 through 64: if you perform services for which you are paid you can earn up to $7,440 a year. Benefits are reduced $1.00 for every $2.00 earned above the limitation. If you are eligible for the maximum Social Security benefits of $12,432, you would lose your entire benefits if you earned more than $32,304.

For ages 65 through 69: If you perform services for which you are paid, you can earn up to $10,200 a year. Benefits are reduced $1.00 for every $3.00 earned above the limitation. If you are eligible for the maximum Social Security benefits of $15,552, you would lose your entire benefits if you earned more than $56,856.

The following table illustrates the effects of the Earnings Limitation.

| Social Security Benefits | | | |
|---|---|---|---|
| **Earned Income** | **Ages 62-64** | **Ages 65-69** | **Age 70 & Older** |
| $ 5,000 | $10,000 | $10,000 | $10,000 |
| 10,000 | 8,720 | 10,000 | 10,000 |
| 15,000 | 6,220 | 8,400 | 10,000 |
| 20,000 | 3,720 | 6,733 | 10,000 |
| 25,000 | 1,220 | 5,067 | 10,000 |
| 20,000 | —0— | 3,400 | 10,000 |
| 25,000 | —0— | 1,733 | 10,000 |
| 40,000 | —0— | 67 | 10,000 |
| 45,000 | —0— | —0— | 10,000 |

**The Effects of Earned Income on**
**$10,000 Annual Social Security Benefits**
**Figure 7-1**

If you are self-employed, you are also subject to the Earnings Limitation until you reach the age of 70. Earnings from self-employment are generally counted when received, not when earned. For the Earnings Limitation, the profits and losses of all your businesses are added together to determine your earnings for the year.

## Self-Employment Tax

If you are self-employed, you must also pay Self-Employment Tax which is the equivalent to F.I.C.A. withholding paid by you and your employer if you work for someone else.

In 1992, this tax is calculated at 15.3 percent of earnings up to $55,500, plus 1.45 percent of earnings over $55,500 up to $130,200. When you calculate net profit, half of the tax is deductible as a business expense. The following table shows what this tax can amount to:

| Income | Self-Employment Tax |
|---|---|
| $ 10,000 | $ 1,530 |
| 15,000 | 2,295 |
| 25,000 | 3,825 |
| 50,000 | 7,650 |
| 75,000 | 8,773 |
| 100,000 | 9,136 |
| 130,000 | 10,658 |

**Self-Employment Tax on Selected Levels of Income**
**Figure 7-2**

## CONCLUSION

Whether motivated by financial or emotional reasons, many people find that income producing activities may be what they need to have a fulfilling retirement.

Changing demographics and federal legislation have helped open up opportunities to older workers. Today, with fewer teenagers in our society, older workers are increasingly filling full-time and part-time positions in the retail, fast food and hotel industries. Employers are finding that they are getting a bargain in the process. Older workers bring expertise, stability and reliability to the workplace—attributes not generally present in teenagers.

As you consider the type of income-producing activity that might be right for you, first consider your needs and the skills you have to offer. Then look at how much time you want to devote to generating income. Consider what you may have aspired to, but not yet attained. These considerations will help you decide among the choices of full-time employment, traditional part-time employment, working through a temporary help agency, or operating your own consulting practice, home-based business or full-fledged business.

As you decide upon your course of action, carefully consider the cost to you of potentially losing part or all of your Social Security Benefits and the cost of Self-Employment Taxes. When these costs are added to state and federal income taxes, you may decide that it is not worth working for the small net income.

Regardless of the activity you choose to get involved in, tell everyone you come in contact with about your interest. Networking is the primary means of either landing a job or finding clients or customers for independent ventures.

# Chapter 7

# *Volunteer Activities*

Annie Mae Searles, at age 86, maintains a truly remarkable level of volunteer service. This former English, Spanish, and Journalism teacher was instrumental in developing an adult learning center where she tutors adults whose native language is not English. She serves as a guide at the Rogers Historical Museum and is secretary of the Benton County Historical Society. She works the polls on election day and takes her turn as hostess at the Apple Spur Community Dinner. She is a member of the Garden Club and visits at the local nursing home. When she isn't busy doing something else, she occupies her time collecting stamps, writing in her journal, and working with her computer.

*Rural Arkansas,* September 1992

If your financial needs are being met so that you are not interested in working for pay, volunteer service may be right for you. Those things you enjoyed most about work, such as interacting with others, working together toward a common goal, meeting challenges and accomplishing objectives, return when you get involved in volunteer activities. The loss of identity you may have felt when you left the workplace, and the lack of structure in your day vanish, while a new sense of purpose and direction takes over.

Volunteering is a popular choice among retirees. Consider the following:

- In 1987, 137 million people gave 19.5 billion hours of volunteer service, valued at about $150 billion.

- According to a 1988 Gallup poll, 47 percent of respondents, between the ages of 55 and 64, do volunteer work, as do 40 percent of those between ages 65 and 74.

- An AARP survey found that 20 percent of those who did not volunteer were interested in doing so.

The active years of retirement provide the greatest opportunities to focus your energies on what means the most to you. What would you like to change in the world? What legacy would you like to leave? These are questions that guide many into volunteer service. As a result of your career, you have a wealth of knowledge and skills to use in meeting the challenges facing our nation—challenges like crime, hunger, homelessness, disease, destruction of the environment, and illiteracy.

As a retiree, you make an excellent volunteer. You have the time flexibility to schedule around the cause you serve. You are dependable and loyal, with a sense of responsibility. You have skills, knowledge, experience and expertise from which to draw, and the wisdom and understanding to view your role realistically.

Approach volunteer work as professionally as you did your career. Look around before you decide where you want to work. Interview the staff and observe as much about the facility and program as you can. You will need to find out such things as what your duties and responsibilities will be, to whom and where you will report, how much time you are expected to put in, whether any of your expenses will be reimbursed, whether training will be provided, whether you will be covered under the agency's liability insurance. If you will be transporting clients in your own car, clarify your coverage with your insurance agent. Check with your accountant or the local IRS office to determine whether any of your expenses incurred in volunteer service are tax-deductible.

There are many kinds of volunteer opportunities, from highly organized national programs, to individual efforts. The kinds of work and types of settings are as varied as the world's problems. The key to a rewarding volunteer job is finding one that combines your specific skills and interests. Is there a problem you want to take on, or a group of people you wish to help? Is there something you have always wanted to do, but never had the time? What skills do you have to offer? Do you prefer to work in a structured environment or on your own? In what type of setting do you prefer to work? Do you prefer administrative work or direct client contact? Your answers to these questions will steer you to the right volunteer opportunity for you.

Approach volunteer service with realistic expectations or you will be disappointed. Most volunteer service takes place in the nonprofit world. If you come from a business or corporate career, you may find many things missing that you took for granted. Adequate facilities, secretarial help and equipment are often in short supply.

---

**Potential Volunteer Involvement**

1. What volunteer service are you involved with that you wish to continue in retirement?

   _____

   _____

2. What cause would you like to work for?

   _____

   _____

3. What age group do you prefer to work with?

   _____ Pre-school children       _____ Mature adults

   _____ School age children       _____ The elderly

   _____ Teenagers                 _____ Family units

   _____ Young adults

4. What type of involvement do you prefer?

   _____ Client service            _____ Board of Directors

   _____ Administrative Support     _____ Fund Raising

Organizations need volunteers who take their duties seriously, who get the job done, and who see that someone else will carry on when they are unavailable.

If you do not take your volunteer assignment seriously and approach it with this level of commitment, it will have little meaning for you and little value to those you serve. To get the most from volunteer service, you need to view your job with the same importance as a paid position.

## VOLUNTEER OPPORTUNITIES

Opportunities for volunteering abound in every community. Whether you prefer working directly with the people being served or behind the scenes in administration, many organizations need your services. And, everyone can use help with fund raising.

### Hospitals and Schools

You need not look any further than your local hospital or school to find interesting jobs. Hospital volunteers work as friendly visitors, nurses' aides and recreation leaders. They bring library carts to patients' bedsides, write letters for patients, work in the gift shop, wheel patients for x-rays or treatments, and assist in clerical duties. School volunteers work as teachers' assistants, tutors, playground attendants and clerical assistants in libraries, bookstores, cafeterias and offices.

### Religious Organizations

Religious organizations have highly organized programs to meet the needs of their communities, including assistance to children, the homeless and the homebound. Religious organizations also offer foreign opportunities in missionary work. Assignments, from one week to two or more years in duration utilize all types of skills. Often these assignments afford excellent opportunities to combine travel and volunteer service.

## Social Service Agencies

Social service agencies need help with programs from caring for AIDS-infected newborns to drug and alcohol abuse counseling, crisis intervention, pre-school care, job development, and assisting the elderly and people with disabilities. Social service agencies are generally members of the local United Way. By perusing United Way literature, you can become familiar with the vast array of opportunities in your community.

## Political Parties

If you are politically minded, consider working for a political party or candidate. You can also get involved in voter registration, special interest lobbies, and consumer advocate groups. Involvement in these activities can lead to opportunities for service to your party, including serving on precinct, county and state committees, and serving as a state delegate to national conventions.

### How to Run for Office

If you think you'd like to run for public office, here's some advice for putting together a successful campaign—provided by Marc Caplan of the Northeast Citizen Action Resource Center.

1. Understand why you want to run. You need to be clear as to why you want to hold office and what you will do to make a difference in people's lives.

2. Be sure you're ready. Running for office is a major step. You may need to rearrange your schedule. Certainly you must work through any potential strains on your family life. If you anticipate these things, life down the campaign road will be a lot smoother.

3. Assess which office you want to run for. Pick an office you really want and have a chance of winning. Can you make an effective case as to why the person who now holds that office should be replaced? Would a Democrat have a chance of winning? How about a Republican? Who are your potential opponents and what are their strengths and weaknesses?

4. Learn about community issues. You don't need to become an instant expert, but you need to have a basic knowledge about what's important to the voters you want to represent.

5. Identify issues you care about and work actively for them. Get involved in community and civic groups working on issues that interest you. Consider going door-to-door with a petition. Write letters to the editor. Speak up at hearings of the city council, zoning board, and state legislature.

6. Contact the political party of your choice and community leaders. Unless you run as an independent, you'll need the support of a political party. Approach party leaders and discuss your potential candidacy. Become active in party activities. Also talk to community and organization leaders.

7. Write a campaign plan. You'll have a much greater chance of success if you have a road map of how to run your campaign. Enlist the help of experienced political hands. Here is where political coalitions are helpful.

8. Form an advisory committee. Identify a small group of close friends who are able to offer ideas and make decisions about campaign activities.

9. Build a list of supporters. Make a long list of friends and associates who can work on your campaign. They don't have to be "political"—you'll be suprised how many social friends will become dedicated campaign workers.

10. Identify how you can raise money. Determine the amount you'll need to run a reasonable campaign. After putting together a list of potential contributors, develop a realistic plan to raise that money.

## Community Service

Community service is carried out through a variety of organizations, including the Chamber of Commerce and appointments to city or county committees, commissions, boards and task forces. Community service can also be performed through election to public office on your local school board, city council and county board of supervisors. Service organizations such as the Lions Club, Kiwanis Club and Rotary International are heavily involved in community service. Finally, your local emergency medical corps, volunteer fire department, search and rescue team, and police auxiliary offer ways to contribute special talents and interests to your local community.

## Cultural Organizations

Cultural organizations offer opportunities for contributing to the arts. Museums, libraries and performing arts centers look for tour guides, ushers and other volunteers to perform a variety of services. Those involved with these organizations have the opportunity to enjoy the services without cost.

## Business Consulting

Business consulting to small businesses and nonprofit organizations is a rewarding way to stay busy, stay involved in the business world, and share your knowledge with those who need it. This activity can be similar to holding a regular job. You do what you know best—give advice based on your expertise.

## Environmental Activities

If saving the environment is your cause, look into recycling programs, activist organizations, or animal rights groups. Parks, zoos and gardens always welcome volunteers. You need not limit your activities to organized groups. Your contribution could be picking up trash or planting flowers along the trail you walk for your daily exercise.

## Professional Societies

If you have been active in your professional society during your career, there is no need to give it up in retirement. Staying active allows you to keep abreast of developments in your profession and to maintain contacts with people with similar interests. Volunteer opportunities exist through serving as an officer, on the board of directors, on committees, and as a workshop or seminar leader.

## Boards of Directors of Nonprofit Organizations

Qualified individuals can serve on boards of directors of nonprofit organizations. If you are recruited for this type of volunteer service, you will have several important responsibilities:

- You will have fiduciary authority and liability for all business operations. Therefore, you must learn to read and understand financial statements.

- Visit programs and become familiar with the group's work. Do not spend all your time in meetings. Get to know the staff, other volunteers, and service recipients.

- Participate in fund raising. Even if you do not have money to give, your responsibility is to persuade others to give. Board members must either give or get the money needed to operate the organization's programs.

- Involve family members. When everyone shares in the responsibilities, they can all share in the pride of achievement.

## HOW TO GET INVOLVED

If you are interested in volunteering but do not know where to begin, one of the best ways is to ask. This sounds simple, and it is. Identify the type of cause you would like to support and the skills you have to offer; then contact the cause that interests you. More often than not, organizations are eager to find volunteers and will be pleased when you approach them. If your interests are with local groups such as nursing homes, hospitals and schools, speak to administrators or public affairs

## Checklist of Potential Service

*Instructions:* Place a check mark under the type of volunteer service that interests you, associated with the causes you choose to support.

| Cause | Client Service | Administrative Service | Fund Raising | Board of Directors |
|---|---|---|---|---|
| Hospitals | | | | |
| Schools | | | | |
| Religious Organizations | | | | |
| Social Service Agencies | | | | |
| Community Service | | | | |
| Political Organizations | | | | |
| Cultural Organizations | | | | |
| Business Consulting | | | | |
| Environmental Protection | | | | |
| Professional Society | | | | |
| Other: | | | | |
| | | | | |
| | | | | |

staff. If your interests are with national organizations, first contact the local offices. If you cannot contact anyone locally, try national headquarters. Most organizations will be pleased to put you in touch with the person or department in charge of volunteers.

## Local Contacts

Almost every town has an agency that serves as a clearinghouse for local volunteer opportunities. Check with your mayor's office or Chamber of Commerce for your local voluntary action center or bureau. Listings in your local telephone book yellow pages may be found under the key words "volunteer" or "voluntary." Religious organizations, civic associations and the United Way are also good sources for referrals.

If these courses do not turn up the volunteer opportunity you seek, write to one or more of the following organizations:

## The National VOLUNTEER Center

The National VOLUNTEER Center supports local volunteer centers that serve as clearinghouses of volunteer opportunities. They can refer you to your local center and provide you information booklets on volunteering:

> The National VOLUNTEER Center
> 1111 North 19th Street, Suite 500
> Arlington, VA 22209

## American Association of Retired Persons (AARP)

AARP operates a Volunteer Talent Bank that matches volunteers and organizations. Many volunteers work in the variety of programs AARP sponsors, providing information and counseling on housing options, retirement planning, widowhood, tax preparation, and health, legal and financial issues. After completing a registration form, volunteers are told about opportunities in their communities.

AARP also publishes several booklets that address the issues of volunteerism:

- Volunteer Talent Bank (D12329)

- Community Service Project Packet (D13669)

- To Serve Not To Be Served (D12028)

- Volunteer Opportunities in Your Congregation (D12612)

- Making America Literate: How You Can Help (D12755)

> Fulfillment Center
> American Association of Retired Persons
> 601 E Street NW
> Washington, DC 20049

## ACTION Volunteer Agency

Today, more than a half million volunteers serve in ACTION programs, confronting such problems as illiteracy, homelessness, drug abuse, abused and abandoned children, and the needs of the homebound elderly. The majority of these volunteers are older Americans. For information on ACTION programs of interest to you, contact the regional recruiting office nearest to you:

10 Causeway Street
Room 473
Boston, MA 02222-1039

6 World Trade Center
Room 758
New York, NY 10048-0206

10 West Jackson Boulevard
6th Floor
Chicago, IL 60604-3964

101 Marietta Street NW
Room 1003
Atlanta, GA 30323-2301

211 Main Street
Room 530
San Francisco, CA 94105-1914

1100 Commerce Street
Room 6 B 11
Dallas, TX 75242-0696

Federal Office Building
Suite 3039
909 First Avenue
Seattle, WA 98174-1103

Executive Tower Building
Suite 2930
1405 Curtis Street
Denver, CO 80202-2349

U.S. Customs House, Room 108
2nd & Chestnut Streets
Philadelphia, PA 19106-2912

*National Headquarters*
1100 Vermont Avenue NW
Washington, DC 20525

The following four ACTION programs are of particular interest to older volunteers:

- *Retired Senior Volunteer Program (RSVP):* This is the largest ACTION program. It provides opportunities to people 60 years and older, through grants to public and nonprofit organizations. Transportation and on-duty accident and liability insurance are provided. Volunteers are reimbursed for meals and expenses.

- *Volunteers in Service to America (VISTA):* This is the domestic equivalent of the Peace Corps. VISTA requires a full-time commitment; volunteers live and work among the poor, in urban and rural areas and on Indian reservations in the U.S., Puerto Rico, Guam, and the Virgin Islands. Training is provided, and a monthly allowance is paid, to cover housing, food, medical care and travel expenses. Upon completing an assignment, volunteers receive a modest compensation for each month they have served.

- *Senior Companion Program (SCP):* Senior Companions help their peers maintain their independence. They are a vital link between elders in need and the community services and resources that make a difference in their lives. Forty hours of training prepare senior companions to work four hours a day, five days a week, on a year-round basis. Volunteers receive a nontaxable annual payment for their services, which does not affect their Social Security benefits. They are reimbursed for transportation and meals, and are provided on-duty insurance and an annual physical exam.

- *Foster Grandparents Program (FGP):* Foster Grandparents provide companionship and guidance to two assigned "grandchildren." Low income persons, 60 years and older, are eligible to become Foster Grandparents to institutionalized retarded, emotionally disturbed, physically handicapped, troubled or abandoned children. After forty hours of training, volunteers are assigned to supervised child-care teams. They receive a modest tax-free income and transportation allowance as well as hot meals, accident and liability insurance and an annual physical examination.

## Team Work

Team Work is a project of the Foundation for Exceptional Children. It serves young people, between eighteen and twenty-five years old, who have learning disabilities, physical impairments, sensory limitations or mild mental retardation. Volunteers serve as mentors and job coaches.

Team Work
Foundation for Exceptional Children
1920 Association Drive
Reston, VA 22091

## Family Friends Project

This project of the National Council on Aging trains volunteers, 55 years and older, to help families who have children with chronic illnesses or disabilities. Volunteers spend a minimum of four hours a week in the familys' homes as companions for the children and helpers for the parents.

Family Friends Project
National Council on Aging
409 Third Street SW
Washington, DC 20024

## Court Appointed Special Advocates (CASA)

Both federal and state laws require judicial review of foster-care cases. CASA volunteers serve as investigators for the court, gathering information on one or two assigned foster-care children. While carrying out these duties, the volunteers become aware of and respond to the special needs of the children they serve. CASA volunteers are trained and supervised by professional staff. Objective and independent thinking, good communications skills, impartiality, sensitivity, dedication to doing a thorough job, and the ability to remain active throughout a case's entire litigation period are required.

National CASA Association
2722 Eastlake Avenue East
Seattle, WA 98102

## Legal Counsel for the Elderly

Sponsored by AARP, Legal Counsel for the Elderly checks on how well court-appointed guardians are taking care of the people under guardianship and report back to the court on the quality of care they receive.

> Legal Counsel for the Elderly
> American Association of Retired Persons
> 1909 K Street NW
> Washington, DC 20049

## National Association of Meal Programs

This is an association of professionals and volunteers who deliver meals to shut-ins. Volunteers receive reimbursement for transportation and meals on the days they work. Typical commitments are for one day a week.

> National Association of Meal Programs
> 204 E Street NE
> Washington, DC 20002

## National Caucus and Center on Black Aged

The National Caucus is a nonprofit organization that works to improve the quality of life for older black Americans. It also encourages the participation of older black volunteers.

> National Caucus and Center for Black Aged
> 1424 K Street NW, Suite 500
> Washington, DC 20005

## American Red Cross

The Red Cross provides food, clothing, shelter and other emergency services to disaster victims around the world. It works to prevent disasters through water safety monitoring, first-aid stations at public events, home health aid, parenting education, classes in CPR, and blood pressure screening. Nearly half the nation's blood supply is collected by the Red Cross. Other programs focus on the needs of military personnel, the young, the elderly and the homeless.

American Red Cross
National Headquarters
Washington, DC 20006

## Peace Corps

Originally a service opportunity for young people, today's Peace Corps
actively recruits older Americans. Volunteers serve two-year terms in
underdeveloped countries, teaching and building essential services for
survival. Living conditions may be rugged, depending upon the
assignment. Training is provided and a monthly allowance covers
transportation, food, housing and medical expenses. At the end of an
assignment, volunteers receive a modest compensation for each month
they have served.

Peace Corps
Public Response Unit
1990 K Street NW
Washington, DC 20562

## Volunteers in Technical Assistance (VITA)

Vita was established by a group of scientists and engineers to provide
technical assistance to developing countries. Volunteers are matched
to requests for assistance in agriculture, small-enterprise development,
housing, sanitation, water-supply management and reforestation.
Volunteers provide designs, analyses, evaluations and guidelines.
Occasional on-site work is required. Volunteers must have technical
skills to share. Most requests are handled by mail.

Volunteers in Technical Assistance
1815 North Lynn Street, Suite 200
Arlington, VA 22209

## Service Corps of Retired Executives (SCORE)

SCORE was established by the Small Business Administration to provide
free management assistance to small business owners. In addition to
one-on-one counseling, they conduct seminars and workshops on

business planning, records keeping, marketing and finance. Volunteers are retired business people with managerial, professional or technical expertise they wish to share with small business owners. SCORE has 387 local chapters.

>Service Corps of Retired Executives
>1825 Connecticut Avenue NW
>Washington, DC 20009

## Executive Service Corps

The Executive Service Corps places volunteers with nonprofit organizations. Volunteers give advice on topics that include long-range planning, finance, administration, marketing, personnel administration, computer applications, facilities planning, budgeting, public relations and office practices. Client organizations include social service agencies, governmental units and universities. Volunteers are reimbursed for out-of-pocket expenses.

>Executive Service Corps
>257 Park Avenue South
>New York, NY 10010

## International Executive Service Corps

For over twenty-five years, the International Executive Service Corps has recruited retired business executives and technical advisors to help companies in developing countries. Volunteers work on assignments lasting two to six months. Spouses are encouraged to accompany volunteers. Travel expenses are paid for both, along with a small per diem. This is a great opportunity to combine international travel and service.

>International Executive Service Corps
>P. O. Box 1005
>Stamford, CT 06904

## Volunteers in Parks (VIPS)

VIPS plays an important part in preserving and protecting our national parks. Volunteer assignments include maintaining trails, counting wildlife, guiding tours, answering mail, maintaining libraries and driving buses. Opportunities vary in duration from a few hours a week, to full-time jobs, either for a season or year-round.

National Park Service
Department of Interior
1849 C Street NW
Washington, DC 20240

## Worldwide Greenpeace Movement

Greenpeace's goal is to preserve the earth and all the life it supports. It works to end the threat of nuclear war, protect the environment from toxic pollution, stop the threat of global warming, and end the slaughter of endangered animals. Greenpeace is an activist movement that believes in nonviolent confrontation. Volunteers assist with member correspondence, maintain press files, do data entry, and prepare and distribute campaign and educational materials. Internships are available in ocean ecology, disarmament, toxic issues, legal issues and the media. Contact the Greenpeace Action Office nearest you:

709 Center Street
Boston, MA 02130

1017 West Jackson Boulevard
Chicago, IL 60607

4649 Sunnyside Avenue N
Seattle, WA 98103

Fort Mason, Building E
San Francisco, CA 94123

Wilton Plaza, Suite 80
1881 NE 26th Street
Wilton Manors, FL 32240

*National Headquarters*
1436 U Street NW
Washington, DC 20009

## Global Releaf

Global Releaf's mission is to combat the greenhouse effect by planting trees. Established by the American Forestry Association, Global Releaf assists individuals, organizations and communities in tree planting projects. Volunteers promote the organization and its goals and organize tree-planting projects.

Global Releaf
American Forestry Association
P. O. Box 2000
Washington, DC 20013

## Sierra Club

The Sierra Club has championed environmental causes for nearly a century. This political activist group pressures for solutions to environmental problems. Volunteers work at all levels of government to achieve the organization's goals.

Sierra Club
Public Affairs
730 Polk Street
San Francisco, CA 94109

## National Audubon Society

The National Audubon Society has been a strong force in wildlife conservation for over seventy-five years. Well respected by government and industry, it is the largest national environmental membership organization. Members work with local communities to save endangered species, protect national areas and wildlife habitats, and develop environmental education programs. Volunteers work through local chapters.

National Audubon Society
950 Third Avenue
New York, NY 10022

## University Research Expedition Program

Volunteers join one or more of the University of California research teams and share in the challenges and rewards of scientific discovery. Expeditions last two to three weeks during the summer. Under the guidance of researchers, volunteers participate in projects ranging from archaeology, botany and sociology to zoology. Volunteers' contributions to their expedition's expenses qualify as charitable tax deductions. Most projects do not require previous experience.

University Research Expedition Programs
Desk L-02
University of California
Berkeley, CA 94720

## Foundation for Field Research

The Foundation matches interested volunteers with research projects around the world. Volunteers need no prior experience. They work under the guidance of a researcher. A field manager accompanies each project handling logistics. Volunteers need stamina for hard work, a time commitment of a few days to a month, and the ability to make a tax-deductible contribution toward the cost of the project.

> Foundation for Field Research
> P. O. Box 2010
> Alpine, CA 92001

## Earthwatch

Earthwatch recruits volunteers of all ages to contribute physical and financial assistance to scientific research expeditions around the world. Volunteers share the cost of expeditions through tax-deductible contributions.

> Earthwatch
> P. O. Box 403N
> Watertown, MA 02272

## American Hiking Society

Each year, the American Hiking Society sends teams of volunteers into parks to help protect and preserve the forests. Volunteers must be experienced backpackers, capable of hiking five to ten miles a day, who are comfortable living in primitive conditions. Teams are made up of six to fifteen volunteers and projects last ten days. Most projects are carried out during the summer; a few go on during spring and fall. Volunteers pay a $30.00 registration fee and supply their own equipment and transportation to the project launch site. Expenses are tax-deductible.

> American Hiking Society Volunteer Vacations
> P. O. Box 86
> North Scituate, MA 02060

## Heifer Project International

Through the Heifer Project, needy farmers in the U.S. and abroad are supplied food-producing animals and taught how to care for and manage them. The animals include dairy and beef cattle, goats, sheep, pigs, rabbits, chickens, honeybees, fish, camels, buffalo and yaks. Each person helped must pass on an offspring of his animal to a needy neighbor. Volunteers are welcome to spend a week at Heifer Project's ranch in Berryville, Arkansas, tending the animals, repairing facilities, cooking or conducting tours. Comfortable housing and rewarding work are available on the 1,225-acre ranch.

> Heifer Project International
> Route 2, Box 33
> Berryville, AR 72126

## Habitats for Humanity

Habitats for Humanity buys vacant lots from cities for $1.00. These lots have been repossessed for default on tax payments. Volunteers build a new house, under the supervision of a licensed contractor. Some work is hired, such as plumbing and heating; companies often donate materials. The future owner must contribute 250 hours of work on the project to be eligible to buy it with a no interest loan when it is finished. Habitat personnel inspect the home periodically, after the new owner moves in, to be sure it is being maintained. If the property is neglected, it is repossessed and resold. Habitat volunteers also go to disaster areas to provide shelter for homeless victims. The international program builds one home overseas for *every* one built in the U.S. Volunteers pay their own tax-deductible expenses. Housing is arranged at work sites at minimal or no cost. Meals are often provided by local organizations.

> Habitats for Humanity
> Habitat & Church Streets
> Americus, GA 31709

## Service Civil International (SCI)

SCI promotes world peace, bringing volunteers from around the world to work on projects in the U.S. and Europe. Work, done in work camps between July and September, lasts between two and four weeks. All work is either social service or scientific. SCI provides room and board during the camp. Volunteers pay their own transportation and out-of-pocket expenses. For information, send $3.00 and a business-sized, self-addressed stamped envelope to:

Service Civil International
Route 2, Box 506
Innis Free Village
Crozet, VA 22932

## Global Volunteers

If you would like to combine volunteer service with your trip to Europe, join Global Volunteers in teaching English to elementary, secondary, and college students at a language camp in Poland. No teaching experience is required. Teams are needed for three-week camps held in a traditional manor house at Siedlice about two hours east of Warsaw, during August, September, and October. Classes are conducted in one to three-hour sessions, but volunteers are given evenings and weekends off.

The tax-deductible cost is $1,525 for three weeks' food, lodging, ground transportation, and project costs. Air fare is extra. Contact:

Global Volunteers
375 East Little Canada Road
St. Paul, MN 55117

## BARTERING YOUR VOLUNTEER SERVICE

Edgar Cahn, a professor at the Columbia School of Law, with the aid of the Robert Wood Johnson Foundation, developed a system for volunteer service credits. The system exists in Boston, Brooklyn, Miami, St. Louis, San Francisco and Washington, D.C.

Sponsored volunteer organizations provide health care services to help the elderly remain in their homes. Services include hospice care, personal care, household service, telephone reassurance, in-home visiting, hospital visiting, transportation, shopping, counseling, escort service, and language translation.

Organizations maintain a record of each volunteer's hours of service, as credits for later use, as needed. Volunteers establish a bank account of hours, rather than dollars. Credits are cashed in by contacting a program manager. People who earn volunteer credits do not feel they are receiving charity when they spend their credits for assistance.

Volunteers like the program and participating organizations report a lower dropout rate than for conventional volunteer programs. For information about a service-credit volunteer program in your area, contact the Robert Wood Johnson Foundation at (609) 452-8701 or write:

> P. O. Box 2316
> Princeton, NJ 08543-2316

## CONCLUSION

Volunteering can give you all the benefits, and more, of holding a regular job. You stay involved, meet new people, use your skills and talents, and you have the added bonus of helping others. It is a great combination. Volunteers perform important services for the community and the nation—services that would never be performed if people had to be hired to do them, because those in need simply do not have the resources.

If volunteer service is a potential activity in your retirement plan, start by selecting a cause you can support with enthusiasm. Assess the skills you have to contribute. You may decide that you will get involved at a lower skill level than you worked at during your career. That is okay; there is no need to take on more responsibility than you will enjoy.

When you know what you want to do, talk to friends and neighbors about opportunities in your community. Check the telephone directory and make a few calls. Register at your local volunteer talent bank. If these leads do not develop the opportunity you seek, contact the organizations of interest to you that were catalogued in this chapter. Or, visit your local library and seek out other organizations. Those catalogued here are only representative of the variety of opportunities available.

Many retirees combine volunteer service with other activities they enjoy, such as traveling and hiking. Through the many domestic and international organizations, you can select an area to visit or an activity to enjoy and match it with an opportunity for volunteer service.

Sharing and caring benefit, not only those served, but those serving.

# Chapter 8

# *Leisure Activities*

Ed and Myrna Fortner, both in their 80s, have traveled to nearly every part of the world since Ed retired in 1982. They have walked on the Great Wall of China, ridden camels in Jerusalem, and traveled by dog sled in Alaska. They've cruised the Caribbean, traveled all through the Orient, to Africa, Greece, Russia, Europe, and Central and South America.

Mrs. Fortner laughs when asked about such activities at her age. "I guess my problem is I don't have the sense to realize I'm getting old. I've enjoyed adventure since I was very young. And, I still feel young."

*The Best of Times,* by Anita Smith

Volunteer activities, discussed in Chapter 7, focus on doing things for others. Here and in the next three chapters, the focus will be on doing things for yourself—simply because you enjoy them.

Leisure activities are those activities you do for the sheer pleasure and enjoyment of doing them. Most people enjoy some leisure activities throughout their lifetimes. Retirement brings the opportunity to either spend more time doing the things you currently enjoy or to pursue new interests.

Leisure activities fulfill different needs than hobbies. Some satisfy a need to be active socially. Others satisfy a need for adventure. Still others provide an opportunity to relax alone quietly. Choose your leisure activities in retirement to help round out your life. Look at what you miss from work. If this need is not being fulfilled through other endeavors, choose a leisure activity that will bring you pleasure.

If you are not yet retired, use your free time during the last three to five years of your career to try a few activities that interest you. This will allow time to eliminate a choice or two and settle on activities that truly interest you. Subscribe to a magazine or two, read some books, consider taking a class or attending a seminar or workshop, and talk to people engaged in the activities that interest you. All of these can help you map your future.

---

**Possible Leisure Activities**

1. What leisure activities have you done in the past, but got away from perhaps due to family or career demands?

   _____

   _____

2. What leisure activities do you currently enjoy that you would like to spend more time doing?

   _____

   _____

3. What leisure activities have you had an interest in doing, but were unable to pursue because of family or career demands?

   _____

   _____

## POPULAR LEISURE ACTIVITIES

The list of leisure activities enjoyed by retirees is limited only by your imagination. It includes such things as bird watching, reading, playing bridge, traveling, going to plays and concerts, visiting museums, going out dancing, and going to sporting events. Here travel, cultural events, games, dancing and reading will be explored, along with grandparenting, the most popular of all leisure activities.

## Travel

Traveling involves more than the trip itself. Planning the adventure and sharing your experiences with family and friends when you return are part of the total experience. Exploring other places and cultures gives you a new perspective on your life. And, you return home with memories that last long after the trip is over.

Many resources are available and are useful in planning your trip. Travel guides can be found in libraries and bookstores. Travel agents can provide you with brochures and advice on transportation and lodging. State and local offices of tourism, the chamber of commerce, visitors and convention centers, and foreign tourist offices can provide maps, brochures, information booklets, and information on transportation and lodging. Talk with friends and family members who have visited your planned destination—you can learn a lot from their experiences. The addresses for state, local and foreign tourist offices are available through your local library. Also, read the advertisements in popular magazines such as *Sunset, Southern Living* and *New Choices.* Maps for any country can be ordered from:

> American Association of Geographers
> 1710 16th Street NW
> Washington, DC 20009

For trips abroad, you will need a passport and, in some cases, a visa and certificate of vaccination. Apply for your passport at least three months before you will need it. Since a passport is required to obtain a visa, this often means you should submit your application more than three months before you plan to depart. Check with the embassy or consulate of the countries you plan to visit, or contact the U. S. Department of State, to find out their requirements.

Office of Passport Services
Bureau of Consumer Affairs
U. S. Department of State
1425 K Street NW
Washington, DC 20525

***Travel on a Budget:*** Retirees can save ten to fifty percent on airlines, buses, trains, car rentals, hotels, meals and tourist attractions. The minimum age requirements vary from fifty to sixty-five. Other ways to save while traveling are to choose the "off season" and to eat dinner earlier to take advantage of "early bird specials." Consider purchasing an airline, bus or train discount coupon book or pass. Check with travel professionals, friends or your library to learn what is available. For example, some airlines sell coupon books, good for a specific number of domestic and foreign flights. Amtrak has a special train-travel package in the U.S., and the Eurrail Pass is economical for European travel. Greyhound's *See America* promotion allows thirty days of unlimited travel. These organizations offer travel bargains for older travelers:

American Association of Retired Persons
Special Services Department
1909 K Street NW
Washington, DC 20049

The National Council of Senior Citizens
925 15th Street NW
Washington, DC 20005

September Days Club
751 Buford Highway NE
Atlanta, GA 30324

Mature Outlook, Inc.
1500 West Shore Drive
Arlington Heights, IL 60004

A little known way to save on accommodations while traveling is to join a bed and breakfast club. The Evergreen/Travel Club has about 700 members in the U.S., most living in the Sunbelt region; two categories of membership are based on whether you choose to open your home to fellow members. Evergreen members act as overnight hosts, while Travel Club members do not offer their homes but do take advantage of other members' guest quarters. Annual dues are $40 for singles and

$50 for couples. Evergreen members pay $10 nightly for single accommodations and $15 for couples. Travel Club members pay $18 for single accommodations and $24 for couples. Members make their own arrangements from a membership roster. For information, send a business-sized, self-addressed, stamped envelope to:

Evergreen/Travel Club
P. O. Box 441
Dixon, IL 61021

***Traveling by Recreational Vehicle (RV):*** Recreational vehicles are the travel choice of many older travelers. In their own vehicles in North America and in rented vehicles in Europe and Australia, these modern-day vagabonds enjoy freedom and economy not available to other travelers. Not counting the cost of the vehicle, expenses run about a third of what others pay, staying in motels and eating in restaurants.

While freedom and economy are major advantages of RV travel, companionship is its greatest incentive to most who choose this mode of travel; every campsite offers an instant circle of friends. Several clubs support this camaraderie through caravan tours and gatherings. The Good Sams Club has more than 800,000 members who are sworn to come to the aid of a fellow member in distress. The club also offers discounts, emergency assistance, campground directories, trip routing and a monthly magazine, *Highways*. With 2,200 local chapters, there is sure to be one near you.

The Good Sams Club
P. O. Box 500
Agoura, CA 91303

***Single Travelers***: There is no need to stay home just because you are single. You can enjoy the benefits of a travel companion by joining one of the organizations dedicated to matching travel partners; you can feel safer, have someone to share the experience with, and enjoy lower double occupancy rates. Contact one of the following organizations and tell them who you are, where you want to travel, and the kind of partner you would like.

Travel Companion Exchange, Inc.
P. O. Box 833
Amityville, NY 11701

Golden Companions
P. O. Box 754
Pullman, WA 99163

If traveling by RV is your dream, you need never feel alone. Loners on Wheels invites you to travel and camp with them. You will find other older singles in the U.S. and Canada to share your meals and fun, and you will get to know other kindred souls. A monthly newsletter will keep you informed of events and in touch with other single campers.

Loners on Wheels, Inc.
P. O. Box 1355
Poplar Bluff, MO 63901

**Publications:** The *Senior Citizen Travel Directory* by Harry H. Henry is full of useful information, including sources for discounts on hotels, transportation, restaurants and attractions. Various travel options are presented, and a state-by-state listings shows campgrounds, RV parks, tour services and points of interest.

Senior Citizen Travel Directory
663 Carlston Avenue
Oakland, CA 94610

The *Mature Traveler* is a monthly newsletter of information on travel bargains with special discounts to subscribers.

Mature Traveler
P. O. Box 50820
Reno, NV 89513

*The Senior Citizen's Guide to Budget Travel in the United States and Canada* by Paige Palmer (Pilot Books, Babylon, NY, 1991) is a handy reference on how to get discounts on all aspects of travel, including package tours and sightseeing information. Check your local bookstore or order it directly from the publisher.

Pilot Books
103 Cooper Street
Babylon, NY 11702

## Cultural Events

Opportunities to appreciate cultural events are available in nearly every community. Museums, theaters, concerts and tours provide occasions for exploring culture. Discount and free tickets are often available to older people and many theaters welcome audiences at rehearsals at no cost.

Volunteering as an usher is an excellent way to enjoy free theater performances and concerts. Most local theaters and concert halls will welcome your help.

With retirement comes flexibility in the time you have to enjoy many of the things offered in your community. For example, you may find it convenient to attend a matinee performance. Also, you may be interested in attending events in neighboring towns that you were unable to attend while working. Other opportunities exist to combine travel and cultural events by taking tours to New York, London or other destinations. As part of their basic package, cultural tours include tickets to performances.

To get involved in your local community, get on the mailing lists of organizations presenting cultural events such as the Fine Arts Department at a college or university, ballet company, symphony, theatrical group and community theater. Read the entertainment section of your local newspaper and be alert for advertisements of coming events on radio and television.

***Roundabout Theater Tours:*** The Roundabout Theater Company offers tours to London every fall. You get to see the best of London's plays and to participate in discussions with directors, playwrights, actors and critics; you can also tour backstage, shop and sightsee. Roundabout Theater Tours offers tours to other destinations, including performances and visits to cultural sights.

> Roundabout Theater Company
> 100 East 17th Street
> New York, NY 10003

## Games and Puzzles

Games and puzzles offer more than just fun: They exercise your mind. In doing so, they help forestall degenerative changes in the brain associated with normal aging. Games get you in contact with others, which supports your need for social interaction. So, play bridge, bingo, chess, checkers or any other game you enjoy; work jigsaw and crossword puzzles to keep your mind active and have fun at the same time.

If you have difficulty with loss of vision or reduced manual dexterity, you can still play your favorite games. Several companies offer games adapted to your needs. Larger pieces, large print, braille and textured and brightly colored elements aid in identifying and grasping game pieces. Cards, jigsaw puzzles, dominoes, Chinese checkers, checkers, bingo, backgammon, poker chips, Monopoly and many other games are available.

Consumer Products
American Foundation for the Blind
15 West 16th Street
New York, NY 10011

Flaghouse
150 North MacQuesten Parkway
Mount Vernon, NY 10550

Worldwide Games
Colchester, CT 06415

## Bridge

Bridge is the most popular game in the world. More than 12 million Americans play bridge, the favorite activity of older adults. According to the American Contract Bridge League (ACBL), the average age of its 200,000 members is 57. Bridge is fun, inexpensive and challenging. It requires risk, evaluation, judgment and logic. It is a great way to socialize and is enjoyed by people at all levels of skill.

In addition to social bridge with friends and neighbors, you can join one of the 4,200 clubs of the American Contract Bridge League (ACBL) where you will find both friendly games and tournaments. Members receive the *Bulletin* monthly, with information on upcoming tournaments and tips from experts. Members also get discounts on cards, books, and other supplies. As a member of ACBL, you can find games throughout the country. The *Directory of Clubs* will let you know where they are located.

American Contract Bridge League
2990 Airways Boulevard
Memphis, TN 38116

## Chess

The U.S. Chess Federation helps both novices and pros become involved in the challenge and excitement of chess. It has 60,000 members ranging in age from 4 to 104. With more than 1,000 clubs around the country, you will never lack for a partner. You will be teamed with players of your ability level, at a club near you. Also, you will receive opportunities for tournament competition and chess by mail. Members of the Federation receive discounts on products and a subscription to *Chess Life*, filled with lessons, game analyses, tips from masters and articles on such things as chess playing computers. If you never played, you will receive free instructions and tips on how to win.

U.S. Chess Federation
186 Route 9W
New Windsor, NY 12553

## Crossword Puzzles

Puzzle buffs can join with thousands of others who love testing their word skills through Puzzle Buffs International. Members receive a history of puzzles, discounts on puzzle books, and a quarterly newsletter filled with games, puzzles and news.

Puzzle Buffs International
1772 State Road
Cuyahoga Falls, OH 44223

## Social Dancing

Dancing is an enjoyable way to stay active, fit and involved with others. Through the ages, dancing has been a popular forum for socializing. As a young man or young lady, you probably attended dances to be with and to meet others of your own age. The same holds true today. Getting involved in dancing will get you involved with other people.

If you have not danced before or it has been so long you need a refresher course, lessons are available. To get involved, check with friends, the calendar of events in your local newspaper, the yellow pages of your phone book, and your library. You are sure to find the type and level of dancing you will enjoy.

## Ballroom Dancing

Couples have been fox trotting and jitterbugging to big band sound in ballrooms all across America for over fifty years. Some of the old bands still play, and new ones have learned the same music. If ballroom dancing is new to you, you will find classes at community centers, YWCAs and dance schools. Ballroom dancing is a great way to have fun and stay fit. Do not let the lack of a partner keep you away. Ballrooms are still great places to make friends.

***U. S. Amateur Ballroom Dancer Association:*** This national organization unifies numerous amateur ballroom dance groups. It conducts events and dances, including National Dance Week, which promotes special events across the country. Championships to select couples to represent the U.S. at the World Championships are held each year. Their newsletter *Amateur Dancers,* keeps members up-to-date on events. The Association can tell you how to find dance groups in your area.

> U. S. Amateur Ballroom Dancer Association
> 8102 Glen Gary Road
> Baltimore, MD 21234

***Publications:*** *Dancing USA* is a national magazine for ballroom and big band enthusiasts. It will keep you up-to-date on orchestras, ballrooms and dance events. You will learn where to get the latest dance videos, books and shoes, as well as where to dance to your favorite music anywhere in the country.

> Dancing USA
> 10600 University Avenue NW
> Minneapolis, MN 55433

## Folk Dancing

Folk dancing clubs preserve the heritage, costumes, music and dance of various ancestries that make up America. Thousands of people of all ages enjoy square dancing, the most popular form of American folk dance. If you are interested in folk dancing, a modest amount of investigation will bring you in contact with what is available in your community. You will find lessons being taught in community centers, churches and by dance clubs.

Square dancing continues to be a favorite of older dancers. Organized through local clubs, dancers keep up-to-date on the latest moves and participate in district, state and national conventions. Once a year most clubs offer lessons to bring in new members. And, most communities will have at least one singles club. Many square dancers combine travel and dancing by attending one of the many square dance camps offered each summer in scenic areas throughout the U.S. Sanctioned as an acceptable form of exercise by the President's Council on Physical Fitness, square dancing is an excellent addition to your physical fitness program.

*Country Dance and Song Society:* This society is dedicated to the preservation, enjoyment, study and teaching of traditional English and American dance, music and song. Members include recreational dancers, musicians, singers, teachers, callers and dance historians. The society concentrates on social and participatory dance forms including contra, square, reel, clog, English country dance and related music. It provides a referral service with information on events and historical and regional aspects of dance and music. It offers workshops, consultations and leadership training across the country and publishes a newsletter and magazine. It also has a library and sales department through which records, books, videos and other material may be bought by mail. One-week summer workshops in Massachusetts and West Virginia offer lessons and a chance to participate in traditional dance forms.

Country Dance and Song Society
17 New South Street
Northampton, MA 01066

*National Square Dance Directory:* This directory lists more that 10,000 square, round, contra, clogging and folk dance clubs throughout the world. It provides information on festivals, conventions, square dance callers, records, equipment, clothing, publications and organizations. With this directory as your guide, you can tap into one of America's favorite pastimes.

National Square Dance Directory
P. O. Box 54055
Jackson, MS 39288

## Reading

The written word can transport you to different places and times to share the real and imaginary lives of others. You can acquire knowledge or be entertained. The opportunities are endless.

Reading is rated by retirees as their number one choice of leisure activity. The vast public library system, with its inter-library loan and computer cataloguing, makes an abundance of material available. Libraries provide discussion groups, classes, meet-the-author events, poetry readings, and many other kinds of programs. Book clubs bring you the newest and best by mail, and in bookstores—both new and used—you can find books on almost any subject. Loss of vision should not deter you. Large print, braille and talking books are readily available. Classes are available at local colleges if you are interested in knowing more about literature and those who wrote it.

*Great Books Foundation:* This foundation is dedicated to providing people of all ages with the opportunity to read, discuss and learn from the great works of literature. There are no educational requirements for participation. Small groups meet for two hours every other week to discuss the reading assignment. Discussions are monitored by trained discussion leaders. There are fifteen sessions in a series, and five series in the program. The foundation publishes the material in the program in soft cover format and trains the discussion leaders. You can either join an existing discussion group or start a new one. Write to the foundation for information on the program and to receive a list of interested people in your area.

> The Great Books Foundation
> 35 East Wacker Drive, Suite 2300
> Chicago, IL 60601

*Bargain books by mail:* The Strand Bookstore is the largest second-hand bookstore in the country. It has more than two million used, out-of-print, and rare books. Prices are low and the staff can help you find whatever you are looking for. Mail order service puts the Strand in close proximity to everyone. A partial listing is available by mail, or you may call (212) 473-1452 for information.

> Strand Bookstore
> 828 Broadway
> New York, NY 10003

## Grandparenting

According to a popular bumper sticker, *happiness is being a grandparent.* Considering the number of people displaying this message, grandparenting must be everything it is reported to be—a special time of joy and pride, a chance to indulge your children's children as you never would have indulged your own. And, more grandparents are alive today than at any other time in history due to the increased longevity enjoyed by today's older generation.

One essential fact has remained constant about grandparenting: You can make a difference in your grandchildren's lives. Children gain a broader perspective on life by spending time with grandparents. No matter how you act toward your grandchildren, you affect their emotional well-being, for better or for worse.

You need your grandchildren as much as they need your unconditional love. Individuals who allow family ties to lapse end up feeling disconnected, disoriented and old, even when they are physically healthy and mentally active. The earlier in a grandchild's life you establish a relationship and the more time you devote to nurturing it, the stronger your bond will become. Many of today's family situations make grandparenting difficult through divorce and remarriage. Grandparents often become step-grandparents. What happens when your child gets divorced and is not given custody of your grandchildren? Maintaining a proper grandparent role, without having it colored by feelings toward your ex-son or ex-daughter-in-law, becomes a challenge in diplomacy.

Since 1965, half of the fifty states have enacted specific laws dealing with grandparents' custody rights. This is a dramatic change from the past, when parents called all the shots. Should you find yourself denied contact with a grandchild for any reason—divorce, death of a parent, unmarried motherhood or straightforward refusal—check your legal rights. While this may not endear you to the grandchild's parent, it will permit you the access you are entitled to and is important in the child's development.

Even if you are separated by a half century and a whole continent, you and your grandchildren can become good friends. The greatest gift you can give them is your time; the greatest attribute you need is patience. Here are some tips on how to put these two to work and in the process become an important part of your grandchildren's lives.

***Include your grandchildren.*** If you have a hobby or leisure activity that children can participate in, include your grandchildren. Take them fishing, hiking, to the theater, to the zoo, for a walk in the park, to the mall or on vacation with you. Let them help you garden, cook, clean and shop.

*Listen to what they say.* In today's world of either single parents or both parents working, there is often too little time to listen to children. Grandparents are uniquely qualified to take up the slack. Look for prime talking times such as bedtime, mealtime or when you are alone together. Encourage your granchildren to share their joys, concerns and experiences. You can listen face-to-face or if you are miles apart, by telephone.

*Keep in touch.* How close you live to your grandchildren will dictate your method of keeping in touch. If you are unable to visit frequently, become pen pals, exchange audio cassettes, or make videos of you reading a story to your grandchildren, showing them your home and neighborhood, or doing something they might find interesting, such as making the cookies you send along with the video.

*Spend private time together.* When families gather, find time to be alone with each grandchild. Young children enjoy being the center of attention and your genuine interest can cement the bond of your relationships. Older children would also enjoy this special time with you.

Several organizations have developed programs for grandparents to spend time with their grandchildren. You can choose to tour Africa, Europe, Canada or the U.S. You can choose to spend a week in the country at a camp. If you are interested in these opportunities, check with the following organizations:

*Foundation for Grandparenting:* If a week at rustic Sagamore Institute at Raquette Lake in New York appeals to you, this is an excellent way to spend time with a grandchild. Mornings are devoted to joint activities; in the afternoons each age group pursues its own interests. Activities include berry picking, square dancing, hiking, campfires, sing-alongs and discussions on grandparenting issues.

> Foundation for Grandparenting
> P. O. Box 97
> Jay, NY 12941

*The Travelers' Society:* This is a nonprofit, tax-exempt organization with world peace and understanding as its objective. It offers educational trips for grandparents and grandchildren to Kenya, England and Ireland, and the Commonwealth of Independent States (the old Soviet Union). All contributions, membership fees and some travel seminar costs are tax deductible.

The Travelers' Society
P. O. Box 2846, Loop Station
Minneapolis, MN 55402

***The Ticket Counter:*** This travel agency has built a substantial business around GrandTravel. They will arrange independent travel for grandparents and grandchildren, or you may participate in their tours to such places as England, Africa, Australia, France, Holland, Italy, Washington, D.C., Alaska, The American Southwest, and the Western national parks. Each trip includes time for the older folks and children to be with others in their own age group.

GrandTravel
The Ticket Counter
6900 Wisconsin Avenue
Chevy Chase, MD 20815

## CONCLUSION

Leisure activities add a special dimension to retirement. They allow you to have fun doing what you enjoy doing. They make a contribution to a well-rounded life, and often afford the means for social activities, challenge and adventure.

Retirement can be the time to get more involved in the leisure activities you have enjoyed for some time. Or, it can be the time to pursue new interests. As you near retirement, look at what you do during non-working hours. What activities would you like to continue and perhaps spend more time doing? What activites have you gotten away from that you would like to get back into? What new activities would you like to try? The activities discussed in this chapter should provide some alternatives for you to consider.

Do not wait until retirement. Begin enjoying your leisure time today. In the process, explore alternatives you might want to get more involved in after your career. Use vacations to get a taste of travel. Set aside some time for reading. Get involved in a bridge group or dance group. Get out more to cultural events in your community.

You probably cannot build a satisfying retirement on just leisure activities, but they are an important part of a full, well-rounded life.

# Chapter 9

# *Hobbies*

A. Tanner Smith, age 81, published his first novel in January 1992. Set in Mesa Verde, Canyon de Chelly, and Grand Canyon, *The Anasazi and the Viking* is a fictional story in a historically accurate setting. Smith spent the better part of a winter studying the lifestyles of his characters and says everything he's written about their customs and ways of life are true according to what he has read.

Now that his first novel has been published he already has begun research on a sequel.

*Shell Alumni News,* March 1992

A hobby results in an output you can be proud of. It might be a craft item you produce, some artistic achievement, or a collection of something. Leisure activities are enjoyed in the course of the experience, but do not result in a "product." Both are important. Hobbies differ from leisure activities discussed in chapter eight, in the satisfaction experienced from producing something. Both make a contribution to a well-rounded retirement. But, they fulfill different psychological needs.

Whatever interests you purely for its own sake is what you should consider pursuing as a hobby. You do not need to justify your interests to anyone. If it appeals to you, get involved.

If you have not actively pursued a hobby during your career, begin as soon as possible—allow yourself as much as five years prior to your retirement to test out a few options and get settled into one that holds your interest. Subscribe to a magazine in your area of interest. Consider taking a class to learn about a hobby that interests you.

---

**Possible Hobbies**

1. What have you enjoyed doing in the past but got away from due to family or career demands?

   _____

   _____

2. What have you had an interest in doing but were unable to pursue because of family or career demands?

   _____

   _____

   _____

---

A hobby is an excellent alternative to work, for a portion of your time. Through a hobby you can find meaningful use of your time, identity in what you do, and satisfy psychological needs such as achievement. While engrossed in the pursuit of a hobby, you lose contact with the passage of time and shut out the world around you. If you elect to join a group of people involved in the same hobby, you can add a social dimension to your experience.

## POPULAR HOBBIES

The array of hobbies enjoyed by retirees is vast. It ranges from antique and classic car restoration, antique furniture restoration, and antique collecting through gardening, photography, quilting, stained glass, stamp collecting and weaving to woodworking. The general categories of arts and crafts, collecting, gardening, genealogy, writing and the performing arts are presented below in detail:

## Arts and Crafts

Artists and craftsmen express their creativity and individuality through wood, clay, glass, stone, metal, paint and fabric. They take pride in their skill, mastery and accomplishments. They have a special reverence for the things they produce.

Satisfactions can be derived from working with your hands in countless endeavors involving beads, ceramics, jewelry, leather, models, stained glass, fiber and wood. For any medium you choose, you will find instructions, supplies, and others who share your interests are readily available. If you are interested, you will also find opportunities to exhibit and sell your work.

Detailed work may become more difficult with age. However, some simple adaptations can help you overcome the difficulties. To start with, see that your work area is well lit. A floor-stand magnifier, or one worn around your neck, will help if your vision is failing. If your joints and muscles do not work as well as they once did, consider electric tools such as scissors, screw drivers and staplers. If your hands are shaky, pin or tack down your materials. Choose patterns with large areas of color and minimal detail. Use bright colors, thick yarns and large-eyed needles. Use rug canvas rather than needlepoint canvas, and use large knitting needles.

*The American Craft Council:* The American Craft Council is a national, nonprofit educational organization serving more than 35,000 members. It works to encourage craftsmen and foster public appreciation of their work. The Council runs the American Crafts Museum in New York City and publishes *American Crafts* magazine. It maintains a resource library with information on books, videos, periodicals, schools, festivals and individual craftsmen.

American Craft Council
72 Spring Street
New York, NY 10012

***The Elder Craftsmen Shop:*** Located on Manhattan's Upper East Side, this nonprofit organization sells either on consignment or through wholesale purchase. Items are produced at home by craftsmen, throughout the U. S., 55 years or older. Similar shops exist in other cities. Contact the New York shop for information on their location nearest you or how to set up your own Elder Craftsmen Shop.

The Elder Craftsmen Shop
851 Lexington Avenue
New York, NY 10021

***Classes and Workshops:*** Most community colleges offer classes in crafts. Other workshops are offered throughout the country and are advertised in craft magazines. Both beginners and experts can learn, gain hands-on experience, enhance their skills, and enjoy the company of fellow craftsmen through classes and workshops. Here are a few for your consideration:

- *Penland:* In an isolated, rural environment, students receive instruction in bookmaking, ceramics, drawing, fiber arts, glassmaking, metalwork, papermaking, photography, printmaking and woodwork.

  Penland School
  Penland, NC 28765

- *Haystack Mountain:* On an island off the coast of Maine, this school provides instruction in blacksmithing, basketry, graphics, book arts, quilting, and work with materials such as clay, metals, fibers, paper, wood and glass.

  Haystack Mountain School of Crafts
  Deer Isle, ME 04627

- *Arrowmont:* On a wooded hillside in eastern Tennessee, students are instructed in weaving, basketry, quilting, enameling, pottery, tapestry and painting.

  Arrowmont School of Arts and Crafts
  P. O. Box 567
  Gatlinburg, TN 37738

- *Anderson Ranch:* Located in Snowmass Village, students receive intensive experience in ceramics, painting, photography and woodworking.

  Anderson Arts Ranch
  P. O. Box 5598
  Snowmass Village, CO 81615

- *Augusta Heritage Center:* This school focuses on the folk arts including quilting, storytelling, whittling, old-time fiddling, playing the hammer dulcimer, dance calling and clogging.

  Augusta Heritage Center
  Davis and Elkins College
  Elkins, WV 26241

- *War Eagle Mills Farm:* On a 200-acre farm in northwest Arkansas, students learn woodcarving, clay sculpting, arrow making, basket making, photography, chair caning, drawing, stone carving, quilting, stain glass, watercolor and acrylic painting.

  Ozarks Arts and Crafts Fair Association
  Route 1, Box 157
  Hindsville, AR 72738

**Publications:** A visit to your local library and newsstand will give you an idea of the number of books and magazines on your particular area of interest. Here are five of general interest:

- *The Crafts Supply Sourcebook:* This is a shop-by-mail guide with over 2,500 listings giving address, phone number and summary for each source listed. It tells where to find supplies, tools, equipment, organizations and publications for all sorts of crafts. You can buy the book at your local bookstore or from the publisher.

  Betterway Publications
  P. O. Box 219
  Crozet, VA 22932

- *American Art Directory:* This biennial publication lists art schools, including information on scholarships, and organizations and associations, as well as periodicals.

Jacques Cattell Press
R.R. Bowker Company
245 West 17th Street
New York, NY 10011

- *Crafting Today:* This magazine provides instructions and patterns for a variety of crafts, including needlework, woodwork and doll making.

Crafting Today
P. O. Box 517
Mount Morris, IL 61054

- *Workbench:* This magazine features woodworking, but includes related subjects such as stained glass. Articles on techniques and safety are regular features.

Modern Handcraft, Inc.
P. O. Box 5967
Kansas City, MO 64111

- *The Crafts Fair Guide:* Published four times a year, this magazine lists crafts fairs across the country.

The Crafts Fair Guide
P. O. Box 5062
Mill Valley, CA 94962

## Collecting

People collect everything—antiques, banks, beer cans, books, bottles, buttons, both toy and real cars, coins, golf balls, match books, postcards, records, salt and pepper shakers, sheet music and valentines, to name a few. There probably is no item you can think of that someone does not collect. If something has caught your interest and sent you rummaging through flea markets, attics and secondhand stores in search of your treasure, you can find others who share your interest. There are clubs, conventions, exhibits and publications for almost any collectible item.

Your interest in searching out, accumulating, and displaying the items that fascinate you can open up a new world of adventure. You can move beyond seeking and finding to researching the history and background of the objects you collect. You can know the pleasure of showing your collection to schools and community groups and socializing with others who share your interest.

To get started collecting, all you have to do is select a category that interests you and look into it. Your local library is a good place to start. Collector magazines have information about events, organizations and supplies. Get acquainted with others who share your interest. Collector clubs provide opportunities to trade, share information and socialize. Most organizations publish newsletters and hold meetings, conventions and seminars. To locate an organization dedicated to your interest, check the *Encyclopedia of Associations* at your local library. Also, the *Standard Dictionary of Periodicals* is a good source for publications.

Collecting need not be an expensive hobby. Many collectibles are quite inexpensive, while some rare items command handsome prices. Some people collect as an investment—it can be risky, especially for the novice. Before making any major purchase, check with several experts and be careful. There are many scams and false claims about collectibles, such as first-edition plates, spoons, thimbles, dolls and coins. Remember, real investment opportunities are seldom offered through mass marketing.

For ideas to get started, the following publications should be helpful:

- *Collectibles,* by Mariam Klamkin (Doubleday, NY, 1981) identifies more than eighty categories of collectibles, including books, clubs, dealers and repairs.

- *Antiques and Collecting* is a monthly magazine featuring articles on glass and china, political memorabilia, furniture, jewelry, etc. It contains market reports, auction news, show calendars and book reviews.

    Antiques and Collecting
    1006 South Michigan Avenue
    Chicago, IL 60605

- *American Collectors Journal* is a monthly newsletter with information on events of interest to collectors. Feature articles highlight many different kinds of collectibles. It includes a calendar of events and a classified advertising section.

    American Collectors Journal
    P. O. Box 407
    Kewanee, IL 61443

## Stamp Collecting

Stamp collecting is reported to be the most popular hobby in the world, with an estimated 19 million collectors in the U.S. alone. The key to enjoying the hobby is to focus on a type of stamp that holds a particular interest for you. Some collectors, for example, concentrate on the stamps of different countries, or stamps picturing animals, sports, transportation, space, art, etc. Others collect blocks of multiple stamps, printing errors, or first day covers.

Getting started in stamp collecting is quite easy. The post office sells guidebooks, stamp collecting kits, and exhibition cards, as well as stamps. Contact the U.S. Postal Service, Philatelic Division, Washington, DC 20265, and ask to be put on the Philatelic Catalog mailing list. Family and friends can save envelopes for you, you can buy packets of stamps from hobby stores, and classified ads in stamp collecting magazines offer a ready supply.

***The American Philatelic Society:*** This society is the oldest and largest organization of stamp collectors. The many services it offers its members include by-mail use of its library, collection insurance, an intermember buying and selling service, and a subscription to its journal, *The American Philatelist.* There are 700 local chapters and over 100 regional shows are held each year, as well as a national convention. The Society will send a beginner's information packet upon request. Send a legal-size self-addressed and stamped envelope to:

Education Department — R
American Philatelic Society
P. O. Box 8000
State College, PA 16803

***Classes and Workshops:*** The American Philatelic Society, in conjunction with Pennsylvania State University, offers home study and summer courses for stamp collectors. Courses cover such topics as fakes and forgeries, buying and selling, and specialty collecting. Home-study courses are offered for beginning, intermediate and advanced students. For information on seminars, write to the address shown above. For information on home-study courses, write to:

Department of Independent Learning
128 Mitchell Building
Pennsylvania State University
University Park, PA 16802

*Publications:* One of the following publications will keep you informed on prices, market values, new issues, recently disclosed errors or forgeries, shows, auctions and dealers.

Linn's Stamp News
P. O. Box 29
Sidney, OH 45365

Stamp Collector
P. O. Box 10
Albany, OR 97321

Stamps
85 Cantisteo Street
Harnell, NY 14843

## Coin Collecting

Coin collecting is one of the world's oldest hobbies. Today, 3 million Americans share an interest in this activity. As with stamp collecting, the beginning coin collector should concentrate on a particular type of collecting. Perhaps the coins of countries you have visited interest you. Other possibilities include different U.S. coins such as pennies, coins of the colonial era, pre-Civil War coins and commemorative coins.

Coin collecting need not be an expensive hobby. Thousands of coins are available for less than a dollar. Be very careful if you are considering coins as an investment. Before making any major investment, contact the American Numismatic Association for their free consumer alert brochure.

Starting a collection is easy. Check around the house. Almost everyone has a few coins tucked away. Examine your change for coins of interest. Buy a good reference book. *A Guide Book to United States Coins,* by R.S. Yoeman (Western, Racine, WI, 1991) is highly recommended. Hobby shops are good sources of supplies. Also magazines and newspapers run regular columns. Coin clubs in your community provide opportunities to share information and share the friendship of kindred souls. Conventions and shows give you the chance to increase your knowledge and acquire coins for your collection.

***The American Numismatic Association:*** This organization is the largest one for coin collectors. As a member, you can use its library of numismatic material and its coin grading service, attend its twice-a year conventions where you may participate in educational seminars, bid on rare coins, and view outstanding collections. You will receive its monthly journal, *The Numismatist*. The Association offers discounts on insurance and travel and coin grading seminars. For a free booklet, *Coin Collecting,* tips on investing in rare coins, or membership information, send a legal-size, self-addressed and stamped envelope to:

> American Numismatic Association
> 818 North Cascade Avenue
> Colorado Springs, CO 80903

*Publications: Coin World* is a weekly newspaper reporting on the latest trends and issues in the world of coin collecting. It features shows, auctions and clubs and has a classified section listing opportunities to buy and sell all types of coin-related collectibles. They also publish *Coin World Almanac* that includes information on rare coins, investments and market information. *Coin World,* a beginner's guide to collecting coins and paper money, will teach you what you need to know to get started in this hobby. You will learn how and where to buy and sell, what grading is and why it is important, how paper money and coins are made, and how to meet other collectors.

> Coin World
> P.O. Box 150
> Sidney, OH 45365

## Doll Collecting

Doll collecting is reportedly the second largest hobby in the U.S., behind stamp collecting. As with other collections, you need to know as much as you can learn about doll collecting. Read books and magazines, visit museums, and talk with other collectors. Then select an area of specialization. Perhaps you will want to concentrate on dolls made of a particular material, boy dolls, baby dolls, ethnic dolls, dolls of film characters, or even the work of a particular artist.

You can start a collection with the dolls you, family members, or friends have saved. Or, you can search in flea markets, attics, garage sales, auctions, shows, shops and classified ads in magazines and newspapers. Look particularly at appropriateness and authenticity of costumes. And, unlike stamp and coin collecting, you want to collect dolls that have been restored and dressed to appear as close as possible to what they did when new.

Collecting dolls often leads to an interest in the history, design, costuming, construction and reconstruction of dolls. This interest can broaden to include repairing, restoring, and making dolls as well as collecting them.

***The United Federation of Doll Clubs:*** This organization preserves, displays, and disseminates information about doll collecting. The Federation holds regular meetings and conventions and publishes *Doll News.* To locate a club in your area, write to:

United Federation of Doll Clubs, Inc.
P. O. Box 14152
Parkville, MO 64152

***Classes and Workshops:*** Lifetime Career Schools offers home-study training on doll collecting, repairing, making, designing and clothing. It also has instruction on how to operate your own doll hospital. The course includes lesson material, supplies, patterns and a year's subscription to *Doll Doings.*

The Doll Hospital School
Lifetime Career Schools
2251 Barry Avenue
Los Angeles, CA 90064

***Publications:*** Hobby House Press offers books on all topics related to doll collecting, including antique and modern collecting, dressing, and price guides. They also have books on doll making, paper dolls, miniatures, fashion history and Teddy Bears. For a free catalogue, write to:

Hobby House Press, Inc.
900 Fredrick Street
Cumberland, MD 21502

Magazines are excellent sources of information on collectible and modern dolls, artists' dolls, and the making and costuming of dolls. They also have a geographical listing of doll shows and events and classified sections on dolls and supplies. *Dolls* and *Dollmaking* are both published by:

Collector Communication, Inc.
170 Fifth Avenue
New York, NY 10010

For a catalogue of doll supplies including parts, wigs, shoes, eyes, eyelashes and display stands, write to:

Standard Doll Company
23-83 31st Street
Long Island City, NY 11105

## Gardening

Gardening as a hobby means getting involved beyond the routine chores of maintaining your lawn. It means investing yourself in the endeavor to the point where you can experience the pride of accomplishment that comes with a job well done. Whether your interests lie with fruits, vegetables, herbs, flowers or ornamentals, gardening is a hobby that brings you in contact with nature. If you tend an outdoor garden, you can also reap the benefits of a low-impact physical workout. The different types of movement, stretching and lifting tone both upper and lower body, while burning calories.

Those who get immersed in gardening often develop interests in organic fertilizers and insecticides, soil conditions, plant pollination and grafting. Interests in landscape design and land usage are also common outgrowths. Many communities have converted vacant lots to community gardens and landscaped common areas through the work of local gardening enthusiasts, so the limit of your involvement need not be controlled by the size of the space you own.

An area of growing interest to gardeners is raising heirloom flowers and vegetables. Many gardening plants are becoming extinct. Of all the varieties listed in the U.S. Department of Agriculture seed inventory of 1903, only 3 percent still survive. Five percent of seed company offerings are dropped every year. In response to this reality, a growing number of gardeners have become interested in preserving plants of the past and saving old-time food crops from extinction. If you are interested, contact:

- Seed Savers Exchange
  Route 3, Box 239
  Decorah, IA 52101

A four-page brochure describing the organization, its projects and publications costs $1.00.

- The Abundant Life Seed Foundation
  P. O. Box 772
  Port Townsend, WA 98368

A nonprofit organization specializing in heirloom and medicinal plants sells its catalog for $1.00.

Growing old roses is another variation of heirloom gardening. Some varieties can be traced as far back as Roman times. While Hybrid Tea Roses all look pretty much alike, old roses offer great variety in their size, shape and perfume. If you are interested in adding a rose from Empress Josephine's garden to your own, contact:

- The Antique Rose Emporium
  Route 5, Box 143
  Brenham, TX 77833

  The catalog cost is $5.00.

- Heritage Rosarium
  211 Haviland Mill Road
  Brookeville, MD 20833

  The catalog cost is $1.00.

- Heritage Rose Gardens
  16831 Mitchell Creek Drive
  Fort Bragg, CA 95437

  The catalog cost is $1.00.

It is not necessary to own a plot of land to enjoy gardening. House plants can keep your home free of pollutants and fill your need to nurture growing things. Anything from lilacs to lettuce can be grown in containers. Several different plants grown in containers can turn a roof top, patio or window ledge into a delightful haven. The following reference will help you get started.

Container Gardening
Brooklyn Botanic Garden
100 Washington Avenue
Brooklyn, NY 11225

***The American Horticultural Society:*** This society seeks to educate both amateurs and professionals on how to obtain the best results for themselves and the environment. Members receive *American Horticulturist* and *American Horticulture News.* They also have access to a gardeners' toll free helpline to get answers to their gardening questions. Membership includes discounts on books, a free seed program, travel opportunities, and workshops and lectures at the Society's headquarters in Washington, DC.

> American Horticultural Society
> 7831 East Boulevard Drive
> Alexandria, VA 22308

***Classes and Workshops:*** You can get instruction in your own community through nurseries, community colleges and county extension services. The Brooklyn Botanic Garden offers classes, lectures, and tours throughout the year. A subscribing member receives *Plants and Gardens* magazine and a quarterly handbook, *Plant and Garden,* that covers more than 50 gardening topics, from beds and borders to weed control. Members are entitled to a plant information service by mail or phone.

> Brooklyn Botanic Garden
> 1000 Washington Avenue
> Brooklyn, NY 11225

***Publications:*** *Gardening by Mail,* by Barbara Barton (Houghton Mifflin, Boston, 1990) is the definitive source of resources for gardeners. It is a mail-order directory with thousands of listings on everything on gardens and gardening.

*The Gardeners' Supply Catalogue* is filled with tools, supplies, furniture, seeds and other products to meet the needs of indoor and outdoor gardeners and to help protect the environment. Some examples are the easy kneeler which is a sturdy, lightweight frame that lets you lower yourself down for clipping or weeding and push yourself up again without straining your back. Turn it over and it becomes a bench.

> Gardeners' Supply
> 128 Intervale Road
> Burlington, VT 09401

## Genealogy

Genealogy, tracing your family's roots, will take you on a fascinating journey. You will not only document names, dates, and relationships, but you will learn the details of how your family dealt with the challenges of life. You will uncover stories that will direct your vacation travel as you develop your file of old letters, photos, and birth, death, marriage and property records. The results of your effort will be a valued contribution to succeeding generations.

Tracing your roots requires painstaking research. You may discover a source that opens up information on several generations or you may come to a dead-end that will require creativity and ingenuity to overcome. Fortunately, there is help available. Regardless of your family background, there are organizations and societies to help you with your search. Even if you are an orphan and have no idea of your ancestry, there is an organization that can help. There are books, maps, and libraries, as well as computer programs and publications, to aid you in your search.

Start your quest with what you know. Write down all the information you have on your family. It helps to decide to trace either your paternal lineage or maternal lineage first. What was your father's name and the date and place of his birth? List the same for his brothers and sisters. Now go back a generation. What about your father's father and mother and their brothers and sisters? Contact family members for any information and stories they can contribute. Collect copies of any records you can find such as birth, death and marriage certificates, deeds, wills, diplomas and obituaries. The family bible will often contain valuable information. Visit graves and write down inscriptions on grave markers. (Consider taking photographs of them.) Write to churches and synagogues where family members attended, for any records they might have.

When you have run out of leads, turn to government records. Many are kept in local courthouses. Census records, taken every ten years since 1790, show names, relationships, ages, and if an immigrant, the year of arrival and place and date of birth. Records up to 1910 are available to researchers. To investigate relatives born in another country, you can check naturalization records and ships' passenger lists.

*Genealogical Libraries:* The three largest collections of genealogical information are the Genealogical Society of the Church of Jesus Christ of Latter-Day Saints (Mormons) in Salt Lake City, the New York Public Library, and the Library of Congress in Washington, D.C. Other excellent libraries are located throughout the country. To find one near you, check *The Directory of American Libraries with Genealogical or Local History Collections,* by P. William Filby (Scholarly Resources, Wilmington, DE, 1988).

• For a list of services available through the Mormon Church, write to:

> Family History Library
> The Church of Jesus Christ
>   of Latter-Day Saints
> 35 Northwest Temple Street
> Salt Lake City, UT 84150

• Visit the New York Public Library and use its books, pamphlets, maps, letters, diaries, portraits, state and local histories and military records.

> The New York Public Library
> Genealogy Division, Room 315 N-M
> Fifth Avenue and 42nd Street
> New York, NY 10018

• Local libraries are linked by computer to most information available from the Library of Congress. This includes town histories, local histories and family histories.

> Library of Congress
> Washington, DC 20540

The National Archives in Washington, D.C. and its regional branches, maintain records on dealings with the federal government. Census, military, pension, passenger ship arrival, naturalization and land records will be most useful to you. The National Archives also publishes several booklets that will help you in your research, including:

• Aids for Genealogical Research

• Using Records in the National Archives for Genealogical Research

• Guide to Records in the National Archives

- Using Census Records

- Military Service Records in the National Archives

> National Archives Records Service
> General Service Administration
> Washington, DC 20408

***National Geneaological Society:*** Membership in the National Genealogical Society entitles you to a wide range of services. Among these are access to the Society's library, the *National Genealogical Society Quarterly,* and a bimonthly newsletter. Discounts are available for publications and educational services. An annual conference features lectures and information exchange. The Society also provides a home-study course in the basics of American genealogy.

> National Genealogical Society
> 4527 17th Streeth North
> Arlington, VA 22207

***Computers and Genealogy:*** Your home computer can be a valuable tool in your research. You can store, sort, retrieve and print your information. *Genealogical Computing* is a quarterly journal published by Ancestry Publishing. It has articles on genealogy software, reviews of new products, and a special section for beginners. The publisher keeps directories of computer interest groups, data bases, software and electronic bulletin boards.

> Ancestry Publishing
> Genealogical Computing
> P. O. Box 476
> Salt Lake City, UT 84110

Family Tree Maker is a simple, quick software program for creating family trees. You fill in names, dates, birth places, and any other information you wish on a fill-in-the-blanks form. The software then draws family trees with a box for each individual and lines to show relationships. The instruction manual includes tips and sources to help in your research.

> Family Tree Maker
> Banner Blue Software, Inc.
> P. O. Box 7865
> Fremont, CA 94537

Family Roots is a comprehensive genealogy research program for both the beginning and advanced researcher. It can produce four types of ancestor charts and two descendent charts. It is simple to use and comes with an easy-to-follow manual, a toll-free helpline, and mail support.

> Family Roots
> Quinsept, Inc.
> P. O. Box 216
> Lexington, MA 02173

***Publications and Supplies:*** You can write to the following publishers for free literature on the products and services they provide:

- Genealogy Publishing Co., Inc.
  1001 North Calvert Street
  Baltimore, MD 21202

- Genealogy Unlimited, Inc.
  P. O. Box 537
  Orem, UT 84059

- Ancestry
  P. O. Box 476
  Salt Lake City, UT 84110

- Goodspeed's Book Shop, Inc.
  7 Beacon Street
  Boston, MA 02108

***Professional Assistance:*** At some point, you may need to hire a professional to help with your research. If so, be sure to check credentials and reach an understanding on the scope of the research, its probability of success, and cost. The following organizations can help locate a professional to fulfill your needs:

- Association of Professional Genealogists
  P. O. Box 11601
  Salt Lake City, UT 84147

- Board of Certification of Genealogists
  P. O. Box 19165
  Washington, DC 20036

- Accredited Genealogists
  Family History Library
  35 North West Temple Street
  Salt Lake City, UT 84150

## Writing

Everyone has a story to tell, whether it be in poetry or prose, fiction or non-fiction. Some aspire to the recognition and income of a successful author. Others are content to record something to share with family and friends. Whatever your interest in writing, retirement is the ideal time to realize your ambitions.

To get started as a writer, you need very little beyond an idea and commitment. If your goal is a book-length manuscript, begin by outlining it into chapters. Then, each chapter becomes a sub-goal, making the total project seem less overwhelming, and more manageable. Spend time organizing your thoughts and materials; organization and careful editing are key principles in successful writing.

Consider taking a class in creative writing at your local community college. While you may not think of your work as creative, through creative writing you will learn better, more interesting ways to express your thoughts.

***Clubs and Conferences:*** Nearly every community has a writers' club. Check your newspaper calendar of community events or ask at the public library. Not only do club members share ideas and critique each other's work, they also provide friendship and moral support.

Writers' conferences provide excellent opportunities to increase your knowledge or writing and marketing, to make contacts, and to share your work with others. Conferences are held throughout the country, so there is likely to be one in your town or nearby. Conferences are publicized in writing magazines such as *Writers' Digest,* which publishes an annual conference list. Also, Shaw Guides publishes a listing of conferences including activities, facilities, and costs.

Shaw Guides, Inc.
625 Baltimore Way
Coral Gables, FL 33134

Senior Scribes, a network of senior writers, charges no membership dues. The organization provides market information and other helpful data to encourage senior writers.

Senior Scribes
c/o Poverty Press
P. O. Box 2035
Cape May, NJ 08204

**Publications:** Every writer should own a copy of *The Elements of Style,* by William Strunk, Jr. and E.B. White (Macmillan, New York, 1972). Its 78 pages contain humor, wisdom and guiding principles valuable to any writer. Updated annually, *The Writers' Handbook* contains information on how to write, what to write, and where to sell your writing. It is available in bookstores or from the publisher.

The Writer, Inc.
120 Boylston Street
Boston, MA 02116

Magazines are an excellent source of markets, techniques, books, contests and conferences. They will keep you up to date on what is going on in publishing and give you ideas on what to write. Two popular ones are:

- The Writer
  120 Boylston Street
  Boston, MA 02116

- Writers' Digest
  P. O. Box 2124
  Harlan, IA 51593

**Computer Software:** Writing an autobiography can be a satisfying experience and leave a record of your life for your children and grandchildren. *Memories*, a software program designed to help you write your autobiography, asks questions about the main events of your life. It helps you compile your wisdom and experience into a manuscript. The finished product is a book, complete with title page, dedication and chapter headings. It is not necessary to master your computer to use this program: it comes with an easily understood manual and the program itself guides you through the writing process.

Memories
Senior Software Systems
8804 Wildridge Drive
Austin, TX 78759

## The Performing Arts

Too often, people limit their self-expression by thinking of the arts as something beyond them. You do not have to achieve national acclaim as a dancer, actor or musician to get involved with, and enjoy the arts. Whatever your skills level, developing your talents to their limits is gratifying. And, age is no limit to the potential for development.

## Music

Retirement is a great time to take up an instrument or go back to the one you played as a child. You could join a choral group or sing in the church choir. If you cannot find a group in your community, organize one.

**Publications:** According to the American Music Conference, you are never too old to learn to play music. They are so sure of it that they will send you a booklet, *Yes You Can!*, free. Send a business-size, self-addressed and stamped envelope to:

American Music Conference
303 East Wacker Drive, Suite 1214
Chicago, IL 60601

Here are two other publications you might find valuable:

- *Choosing a Music Teacher*, available from:

    The Music Teachers National Association
    617 Vine Street, Suite 1432
    Cincinnati, OH 45202

- *So You've Always Wanted to Play the Piano*, available from:

    The National Piano Foundation
    4020 McEwen Street, Suite 105
    Dallas, TX 75244

**S.P.E.B.Q.S.A.:** If the close harmony and fellowship of barbershop quartet singing appeals to you, you can join a local chorus. The

Sweet Adelines are for women and the Barbershoppers are for men. Check your local newspaper's calendar of community events or write to their national headquarters.

> The Society for the Preservation
>   and Encouragement of Barbershop
>   Quartet Singing in America
> 6315 Third Avenue
> Kenosha, WI 53140

***Amateur Chamber Music Players:*** If you enjoy playing or singing chamber music, the Amateur Chamber Music Players can connect you to other people with similar interests, in the U.S. and in fifty other countries. Membership entitles you to an annual newsletter. The association also publishes a list of recommended chamber music and maintains a music lending library. The library is connected with the inter-library loan system.

> Amateur Chamber Music Players, Inc.
> 545 Eighth Avenue
> New York, NY 10018

***Bagaduce Music Lending Library:*** This library has a variety of music for piano, chamber ensemble, popular vocal music, and sacred and secular choral music with orchestral accompaniment. For a small yearly membership fee, you can borrow music for up to two months.

> Bagaduce Library
> Green's Hill
> Blue Hill, ME 04614

***Workshops:*** One of the best ways to learn new music, meet fellow musicians, and play with others is to attend a workshop or other special event. Every February, *Music for the Love of It* publishes a directory of summer workshops.

> Music for the Love of It
> 67 Parkside Drive
> Berkeley, CA 94705

For a directory of chamber music workshops and summer festivals, write to:

Chamber Music America, Inc.
545 Eighth Avenue
New York, NY 10018

Folk and country music are performed, celebrated and taught by these organizations:

Augusta Heritage Center
Davis and Elkins College
Elkins, WV 26241

Country Dance and Song Society
17 New South Street
Northampton, MA 01060

**Publications:** *Music for the Love of It* is a newsletter for amateur musicians with articles on technique, music interpretation, composition and workshops. Write to the address shown above. *The Musical Mainstream* is devoted to the needs of blind and visually impaired musicians. Articles are available in large print, braille and disc formats. Subscriptions are free to blind and visually impaired persons.

Library of Congress
National Library Service for the
   Blind and Physically Handicapped
1292 Taylor Street NW
Washington, DC 20542

## Dance

Dance is an enjoyable way to stay active, fit and involved with others. It is never too late to learn to dance. The notion that it is an activity reserved for the young, highly trained body is proven wrong every day in communities throughout America. Tap, modern and interpretive are the most common forms of dance enjoyed by older participants. Both groups and individuals find themselves in demand to perform for local TV stations, senior centers, schools and conferences. Getting involved is as simple as checking your community calendar and attending a meeting. You should have no problem locating a group in your community.

**The Dance Exchange:** This organization, in Washington, D.C., sponsors Dancers of the Third Age. Members of this company range in age from 60 to 90. They give performances at elementary schools, colleges, art galleries, senior centers, national conventions, seminars and festivals across the U.S. and in Europe. Members often join with other dance companies when the performance calls for both older and younger dancers. To help expand the opportunity for older dancers, the Dance Exchange offers teacher training courses and assistance to those wishing to implement similar programs in their communities.

> Dance Exchange, Inc.
> 1746 B Kalorama Road NW
> Washington, DC 20009

**Publications:** The National Dance Association has compiled a resource guide for dance music, recording companies, books, journals, organizations and multicultural resources.

> American Alliance for Health,
>     Physical Education, Recreation, and Dance
> 1900 Association Drive
> Reston, VA 22091

## Drama

Drama is a collaborative art requiring the efforts of actors, directors, producers, set designers, costume designers, stage managers, stage hands, lighting technicians, sound technicians, ushers, house managers and box office help. Each of these areas offers you opportunities to get involved. If you like to perform, work backstage, sell tickets, sell refreshments, sew costumes, paint sets, take tickets or show people to their seats, you can find a job that fits your interests. Many nonprofit community theaters depend on volunteers and sorely need assistance. To get involved, contact your local arts council, community theater, community center or area office on aging.

If you desire to perform, go for it. Theater arts are taught at community centers and schools across the country. Amateur theater groups welcome additions to their membership and provide an outlet for your talent. All you need are a belief in yourself and a willingness to work on perfecting your skills.

**H.B. Studio:** H.B. Studio, in New York, in Greenwich Village, is open to serious students of any age and level of development. Instruction is given in acting technique, scene study, script analysis, musical theater, speech, voice, script writing and directing. Low fees make it easy for struggling artists to develop their skills.

Herbert Berghof Studio
120 Bank Street
New York, NY 10014

**Publications:** *A Challenge for the Actor,* by Uta Hagen (Scribner's, New York, 1991) is a synthesis of Miss Hagen's experiences, acquired during a lifetime of acting and teaching. The essential elements necessary for dramatic action are defined and methods for evoking true behavior are explained. *Three One-Act Plays about the Elderly,* by Elyse Nass (Samuel French, New York, 1990) is a book of comedy dramas by the award-winning playwright. Production rights are available from the publisher.

Samuel French
46 West 25th Street
New York, NY 10010

## CONCLUSION

Hobbies add a special dimension to retirement. They allow you to get involved with something for sheer pleasure. Hobbies provide a special satisfaction derived from producing something with your hands and mind that you can be proud of. When you leave the workplace, the satisfaction of your need to achieve can best be obtained through a hobby.

Retirement can be the time to get more deeply involved with a hobby you have enjoyed for many years, or it can be the time to get involved with something new. As you approach retirement, consider how you spend your non-working hours. Do you make room in your schedule for a hobby? If not, what would you like to try? If you have a hobby, would you like to continue with it and perhaps invest more time in it, in the future?

Do not wait until retirement to start a new hobby. Begin now to explore your interest. Read books, visit with others who are active in your area of interest, subscribe to a magazine, and consider taking a class. All of these can whet your interest and get you started in your post-career endeavor.

You are never too old to be creative and productive, and to grow intellectually. Grandma Moses did not start painting until she was past 70. Goethe was 80 when he finished *Faust*, and Oliver Wendell Holmes wrote some of his best work in his 70s.

# Chapter 10

# *Educational Activities*

> Helene Griffin Robertson graduated magna cum laude from the University of Alabama in Birmingham with a degree in English and Latin at age 76. She says going back to college was one of the most enriching experiences of her life.
>
> She didn't plan to graduate when she first got involved. She signed up for an Elderhostel program. After three summers of Elderhostel experiences she knew that she loved being in a college environment and learning. So she moved into a college dorm and became a full-time student.
>
> *The Best of Times*, by Anita Smith

Retirement gives you the chance to look at the world of education with a fresh perspective. You may explore anything you want, at your own pace, for no other reason than your interest in it. You need not prepare for a career, unless you want to. You do not have to earn a degree, unless you want to. You do not even have to take tests, unless you want credit for the class.

While you obtained your early education, you may have been interested in courses that did not fit into your curriculum—courses like philosophy, literature, history, astronomy and zoology. You now have an opportunity to go back to school and study these subjects to your own satisfaction. Or, perhaps you began a course of study, had to drop out before completing it, and always felt a longing to return. This is the time to bring closure to that part of your life by completing the course of study you began years ago. Perhaps your plans in retirement call for getting involved in something new—employment, leisure activity or hobby. You may find additional schooling a necessary prerequisite to getting involved in your chosen activity. Do you need a law degree, teaching certificate, or foreign language, or a manual skill such as auto mechanics, woodworking or quilting?

Older people return to school:

- To learn
- To complete
- To prepare

According to the U.S. Census Bureau, more than 320,000 Americans, aged 50 and older, are attending college classes. The American Association of Retired Persons estimates that 52 percent of those aged 50 to 64, and 35 percent of those aged 65 and older, are in school. By joining these people in the classroom, you can stimulate your mind, come in contact with interesting people, be challenged intellectually, and accomplish something of value. Educational activities fulfill many of the same roles as work. They provide you with identity, structure, social contact and an environment for satisfying your needs.

**Potential Educational Activities**

1. Do you have an educational goal that has not been reached? _____ Yes _____ No

   If yes, what is that goal? _____

   _____

2. What topics would you like to know more about?

   _____    _____

   _____    _____

3. Are you planning a retirement activity that requires you to learn something before getting involved? If so, what do you need to learn?

   _____

   _____

## TRADITIONAL PROGRAMS

You are welcome as a regular student at just about every institution in the U.S. and Canada. And many have set up special deals to lure you back to the classroom. About one third of the 3,200 accredited colleges and universities in the U.S. now formally recognize that older students bring a commitment to education and a depth of experience that enriches the classroom for everyone. This recognition may take the form of lower administrative fees, special courses, and easier access for those who choose to audit classes.

As you plan your re-entry into the world of education, you need to have an objective. This will help you choose among the options available. Community colleges offer one option, while four-year colleges and universities offer another.

## Community Colleges

Community colleges offer four basic tracks of study: the basic education track prepares students to successfully complete the (GED) high school equivalency exam. The vocational skills track teaches students the skills they need to pursue a career when they graduate from the community college. The academic track prepares students to transfer to a state college or university and receive credit for classes completed toward a four-year degree. Finally, the community interest track is where students learn skills in a wide range of topics, from art, dancing and music, to quilting, weaving and woodworking.

Community colleges fill a special need in the educational system. They are readily available to interested students, offer many classes in the evening, are inexpensive and offer non-credit classes generally not available at four-year institutions. The average age of students in community colleges is 38 years old, reflecting their appeal to older students.

Your local community college can be an ideal place to begin preparation for your retirement. Take a course or two to prepare you to enjoy a hobby or leisure activity. Most older students are not enrolled in a degree program. They simply take courses that interest them. Since they are not pursuing a degree, they often audit courses rather than take them for credit.

For general information on educational opportunities for adults, contact:

Adult Education Association of the U.S.
810 18th Street NW
Washington, DC 20036

## Four-Year Colleges and Universities

Retirement is an excellent time to obtain a college degree or to attend classes for the joy of learning. If you ever have, it has probably been a long time since you have had the luxury of devoting your full attention to learning. The opportunity to get back into a classroom, with plenty of time to devote, can be an exciting challenge.

Most colleges and universities offer free or reduced tuition to older students. The minimum age to qualify varies from 60 to 62 to 65, depending upon the institution. To find out what is available to you, request *Tuition Policies in Higher Education for Older Adults*, from the Institute of Lifetime Learning. The Institute is a clearinghouse and research center on education for older learners. It can be a great help in finding out about educational opportunities.

Institute for Lifetime Learning
1909 K Street NW
Washington, DC 20049

## Studying in Canada

Practically every college and university in Canada offers free tuition to students over the age of either 60 or 65. For a charge of $5 or $10 per course, the colleges of applied arts and technology offer credit courses to retirees, through the Departments of Continuing Education or through the Extension program. Older students have the same privileges as everyone else and must follow the same rules. For information, write to the college of your choice. You can preview the various Canadian colleges and universities at your local library and get the addresses of those you are interested in.

## College Credit for Current Knowledge

If you want to earn a college degree, you can receive as much as three years of academic credit for what you already know. Knowledge acquired through life experience, on the job, in the military, and from volunteer work, earlier studies, reading and independent study can be turned into college credit through the College-Level Examination Program (CLEP) and portfolio assessment.

Nearly 75 percent of all accredited institutions of higher learning accept satisfactory scores on CLEP exams as credit. Exams in five areas measure proficiency in English composition, humanities, math, natural sciences and history. Exams are also available to measure your knowledge in thirty different, specific subjects. Exams are given monthly at more than twelve hundred test centers across the country. For information on institutions accepting CLEP exams for credit and the location of testing sites, write:

College-Level Examination Program
P. O. Box 6600
Princeton, NJ 08541

The second way you can earn college credit for what you already know is through *portfolio assessment*. First, talk to a college advisor to find out how past activities qualify for credit. Then, put together a portfolio about your educational goal and what you have learned over the years that will contribute to reaching that goal. The institution will evaluate your portfolio.

In determining how many credits to award for life experience, many institutions follow guidelines designed by the American Council on Education. The Council has issued a series of directories that contain evaluations of thousands of military and corporate courses. If interested, you can usually find these directories at most college libraries, academic deans' offices and registrars' offices.

Clearly, if you plan to earn a degree, make a record of all the courses you have ever taken, for any reason. For example, having a real estate broker's license can be worth three credits. Search your files, your canceled checks, and your memory.

## Financial Assistance

If you are working toward a degree, you may qualify for financial assistance in the form of scholarships, grants, loans or part-time jobs at the college or university. Aid, today, is usually for one school year; you must reapply for the following year. Contact the school's financial aid office to find out what is available.

Public funds are available for displaced homemakers, low-income workers, and people with disabilities. Agencies administering these funds vary from state to state. With perseverance and your telephone, you should be able to locate the person in your area who can help. Start with state departments with names such as education, employment and training, health and human services, and labor.

For information on federal funding, write for a copy of *The Student Guide: Five Federal Programs*:

Federal Student Aid Program
P. O. Box 84
Washington, DC 20044

## NON-TRADITIONAL PROGRAMS

The increase in the portion of the U.S. population over age 65 has spawned some creative ways of combining learning and travel. This has also supported the development of senior learning centers in many states. These innovations in education, coupled with a few that have been around awhile that are not limited to older adult students, present an interesting range of choices. This section will look at home study, travel and learning, and senior learning centers.

### Home Study

If you have the discipline and ability to learn on your own, you can get a college degree without entering a classroom. Several institutions grant associate, bachelors, masters and doctoral degrees through independent study, correspondence courses, and credit-for-life experiences. These programs are known generally as *Universities without Walls*. Some provide structured learning materials or use the technology of computers or VCRs. Others let you design your own program under the guidance of an advisor. Some require a full-time commitment, while others allow you to study part-time, at your own pace. When considering a program of this type, be sure the program is accredited by the National Home Study Council.

Several colleges offer home study degree programs. A few minutes of research at your local library will produce a list of names and addresses. Two examples of accredited programs are:

> Goddard College
> Plainfield, VT 05667

> Ohio University
> External Student Program
> 309 Tupper Hall
> Athens, OH 45701

If you are considering an alternate or external degree program, write to the Council for Adult and Experiential Learning for information. You will find it helpful.

> Council for Adult and Experiential Learning
> 226 West Jackson Street, Suite 510
> Chicago, IL 60606

Home study is used for more than earning a college degree. You can learn a new hobby, get your high school diploma, test your aptitude for a subject, improve your skills as a volunteer, or pursue self-fulfillment. Opportunities are available to study any subject that interests you.

Before signing up for a course, make sure it meets your educational goals. If you plan to apply credit for the course toward a college degree, check with the college to be sure the credit is transferable. If you are seeking a license or certificate, contact the licensing authority to be sure the course is acceptable.

*The National Home Study Council:* The Council is an independent, non-profit organization that acts as a clearing house and advocate for home study. It sponsors an accrediting commission that evaluates home study schools. The Council publishes a free directory of accredited schools.

> The National Home Study Council
> 1601 18th Street NW
> Washington, DC 20009

*Publications:* Two books, available from your library, local bookstore, or direct from the publisher, offer a wealth of information on home study:

- *Home Study Opportunities* by Laurie M. Carlson (Betterway, Crozert, VA, 1989) is an encyclopedic guide to going to school by mail.

  > Betterway Publications, Inc.
  > Box 219
  > Crozert, VA 22932

- *The Independent Study Catalog* (Peterson's, Princeton, NJ 1989) lists ten thousand high school, college and graduate courses offered by more than seventy colleges and universities.

  > Peterson's
  > P. O. Box 2123
  > Princeton, NJ 08543

## Travel and Learning

Combining learning and travel is an ideal way to immerse yourself in an intense learning experience. You will come away refreshed and rejuvenated. There are many programs to choose from. Academic institutions, alumni associations, museums, travel agencies and non-profit organizations offer a variety of short courses in the U.S. and abroad.

Programs vary widely. Before signing up, make sure you know what you are getting into: accommodations range from rustic to luxurious and fees vary from moderate to expensive. Room, board and transportation are sometimes, but not always, included. Here are several popular programs for your consideration.

*Elderhostel:* This educational program for older people who want to expand their horizons offers some of the world's best bargains. From its beginning in 1975, it has developed a network of about 1,000 schools, colleges and universities in all 50 states, in all 10 Canadian provinces, and in more than 35 other countries. The program offers inexpensive, short-term residential learning vacations to persons over age 60 and their companions over age 50.

Each hosting institution is different in location, size, academic orientation and atmosphere. Courses frequently have a regional flavor. You live on campus and take up to three courses from a selection of subjects in liberal arts and science, taught by the host's faculty. There are no educational prerequisites for any of their courses, no exams, grades, homework or credits.

The range of course offerings is impressive, so you are sure to find something of interest. Recent examples at U.S. institutions include Birds of the Southwest, The History of Country Music, The Rise of Western Civilization, Human Anatomy, Ecology of Alaska, Creative Writing, Wines of the World, Appalachian Heritage, Literature of the Holocaust, The Art of Weaving, Indian Pottery of the Southwest, and The Battle of Gettysburg.

Most programs begin Sunday afternoon and end the following Saturday morning. Accommodations range from rustic cabins in the Rockies to urban high-rises at city universities. Students dine on campus food and are eligible to enjoy the school's recreational and cultural resources. Costs are remarkably low and include room, board, tuition and extracurricular activities. You pay your own transportation to the host institution.

Internationl programs usually last for three weeks and combine morning classes with afternoon excursions. The campus serves as home base, while you study the culture, history and lore of the land with native instructors. These trips typically include stays at three different campuses and include transportation from U.S. gateway cities.

For information on Elderhostel, and to get on the mailing list for its quarterly course catalog, write to:

> Elderhostel
> 80 Boylston Street, Suite 400
> Boston, MA 02116

*Interhostel:* Sponsored by the University of New Hampshire, Interhostel provides international travel-study programs for people over the age of 50. It offers two-week courses at colleges and universities in Europe, China and Australia. The idea is to stay in a place long enough to learn something about it. During your stay, you will be introduced to the history, culture and people of the country you are visiting, through a combination of lectures, field trips and social activities. Groups are limited to 40 people, accompanied by a representative of the University of New Hampshire.

Living quarters are in residence halls or modest hotels. Most meals are served cafeteria style and feature food of the local region. The cost is moderate for what you get and includes two weeks' full room and board, tuition and ground transporation. You pay your own transportation to the host location, but it is arranged by Interhostel and is the least expensive available.

Recent programs have included England, the Scottish Highlands, Eastern Europe, Ireland, Germany, Puerto Rico, Portugal, Sweden, Switzerland, Spain, China, Australia, New Zealand and Thailand.

> Interhostel
> University of New Hampshire
> 6 Garrison Avenue
> Durham, NH 03824

*Cornell's Adult University:* For more than twenty years, Cornell has been treating adults to a week of college life. This program is the largest, most diverse of its kind in the U.S. People of all ages can participate alone, with a friend, with their children or grandchildren. There are programs for everyone.

The program begins with orientation and a welcome party on Sunday. Classes begin on Monday and are taught by Cornell's faculty. Subjects range from opera to how to succeed in America. In the afternoons, participants are free to enjoy Cornell's athletic facilities, lectures, outdoor concerts, plays, museums and hiking trails. Each evening features a dinner of special interest. The week ends with a banquet, faculty roast and graduation party.

Cornell's Adult University
626 Thurston Avenue
Ithaca, NY 14850

***Travel with Scholars:*** Every summer, the University of California at Berkeley offers opportunities to participate in liberal arts courses utilizing the resources of the world's great cities. You can study art in Paris, Medieval Literature at Oxford, unveil the mysteries of Japanese culture at Kyoto, go behind the scenes of London's theaters, or trace the history of Scotland through its countryside.

All classes are taught in English, by members of Berkeley's faculty. Advanced reading is required and college credit is available.

University of California Berkeley Extension
2223 Fulton Street
Berkeley, CA 94720

***Oxford-Cambridge University Vacations:*** This program is for students of all ages and operates during April, July and August. The organization arranges sessions ranging from a week to twelve days, at either Oxford or Cambridge University. Mornings are spent attending lectures on such subjects as Chaucer's England, the Days of King Arthur and Camelot, Great Castles and Cathedrals, and Medieval Life. In the afternoons, participants can go on excursions and explore the locality. Costs are quite reasonable.

Oxford-Cambridge University Vacations
9602 NW 13th Street
Miami, FL 33172

***Foundation for European Language and Educational Centers:*** At the Foundation's twenty-two language centers in France, Spain, Italy, Germany, Switzerland and Japan you live the language you are learning. Classroom sessions are supplemented with excursions and special events. Most students live with host families.

Programs run from two to twelve weeks. There are no prerequisites. Beginner to advanced level courses are available and students receive an evaluation and certificate when they complete a course.

Council Travel
Eurocentre Department
205 East 42nd Street
New York, NY 10017

*International Friendship Service:* Students attend college in Europe and receive intensive instruction in a foreign language by signing up with this organization. Seminars are held during the summertime and run from one to twelve weeks. There are no age limits for participating. Current programs are offered at universities in Germany, Switzerland, France, Italy and Corsica.

Participants receive many hours of language instruction each week, lodging in student housing or a hotel, excursions, tuition, some meals and some other activities. Prices are low and students pay their own transportation, both to the university and locally. Write for information to:

International Friendship Service
22994 El Toro Road
El Toro, CA 92630

*Saga Holidays:* This 35-year-old British travel firm specializes in travel for people over 60 and their companions over 50. It has expanded into Australia and the U.S., and now is the largest travel firm in its field. Bookings are handled only by telephone or direct mail.

Participants may travel by motor coach, take a cruise, or stay in one location. Saga takes them on African safaris or on tours to the Swiss Alps, the Great Smoky Mountains, or great gardens of the East Coast. Saga recently teamed up with the Smithsonian Institution to offer educational tours and cruises. For information, write to:

Saga Holidays
120 Boylston Street
Boston, MA 02116

*Close Up Foundation:* The Close Up Foundation is a nonprofit, nonpartisan organization. In cooperation with the American Association of Retired People, it has brought more than 160,000 people to

Washington, D.C. to study government. They offer educational vacations for people ages 50 and older, where they receive a week of "inside" Washington. Activities include two or three seminars a day on topics of current concern, daily briefings, tours of the city, a day on Capitol Hill, an evening at the theater, daily workshops, a banquet, and some scheduled free time. Considering what you get, the price is remarkably inexpensive.

>Close Up Foundation
>1235 Jefferson Davis Highway
>Arlington, VA 22202

*Publications:* Three books will be very helpful to you as you plan your travel/learning adventures. Copies are available from your library, local bookstore, or directly from the publisher.

- *The Guide to Academic Travel* is a one-stop resource listing hundreds of programs at colleges, universities, museums and other organizations.

>Shaw Guides, Inc.
>625 Biltmore Way
>Coral Gables, FL 33134

- *Travel and Learn: The New Guide to Educational Travel* describes more than a thousand vacation programs offered by 162 colleges, universities, museums and other educational institutions in the U.S. and abroad.

>Blue Penguin Publications
>147 Sylvan Avenue
>Leonia, NJ 07605

- *Learning Vacations* is a guidebook to over 400 learning vacation opportunities.

>Peterson's
>P. O. Box 2123
>Princeton, NJ 08543

## Senior Learning Centers

Many colleges and universities offer special programs for older adult students. These programs offer a relaxed environment, free from the pressure of grades and tests, where you can enjoy an exchange of ideas and social activities with your peers.

Some programs are academically oriented, while others focus on practical or recreational subjects. Some combine both. Many programs involve students in decisions on subjects to be offered, teaching classes, and acting as discussion leaders and resource people. Other programs are planned by the continuing education department and may be taught by paid instructors with input from students as to courses to be offered.

Most programs include the full use of the school's facilities, such as the library, cafeteria and recreational areas. An opportunity to participate in the cultural life of the institution is an added benefit; this may include concerts, plays, lectures and films. Program participants often plan their own group activities such as tours, luncheons, and discussions.

Generally, programs do not have entrance requirements. However, a few programs geared to retired professionals may require committee approval. Fees range from nothing to several hundred dollars a semester.

The following examples of senior learning centers will give you an idea of what is available. For a complete listing, write for *College Centers for Older Learners*, which contains a state-by-state rundown of programs designed specifically for older adult students. The listing includes 254 peer-taught and continuing education programs.

> Institute of Lifetime Learning
> 1909 K Street NW
> Washington, DC 20049

***The Institute for Retired Professionals:*** This is the original senior learning center, begun in 1962 and located at the New School for Social Research in New York City. The Institute brings about 650 retired professionals together to develop their own educational community. Participants expand and enhance their own educational development by sharing experiences, knowledge and skills with others in the community.

The community is sub-divided into approximately 80 study groups, centered around topics of interest to the participants. Topics range from literature, art, music, history, languages, psychology and public affairs to writing, painting and ceramics. Groups are led by members of the community who design the course and lead discussions. Leaders are not experts, but are engaged in the learning process. During discussions, groups draw heavily on the background of participants.

Social activities are also part of the Institute's program. Tickets to cultural events such as plays, concerts and dance programs are available to members. Trips to museums, gardens and cultural attractions are planned each semester. Participants are entitled to full library privileges and use of the school's cafeteria.

Each year the Institute publishes a review containing poems, essays, short stories, illustrations and photographs created by participants. There is also an annual art show exhibiting the work of painters, sculptors, ceramists, collagists and photographers. The lounge features the art work of a different artist each month, allowing many exhibit opportunities.

Each person is both a student and teacher, and shares the responsibility of maintaining the intellectual climate of the Institute. Everyone participates in the organization, design and format of the curriculum. Policies are formulated by a twelve-member council elected by the members, and a director appointed by the New School. Eight standing committees help run the affairs of the Institute.

Membership is open to anyone recently retired from a profession or executive career. Applicants are interviewed by an admissions committee member and must have the committee's approval for admission.

> Institute for Retired Professionals
> New School for Social Research
> 66 West 12th Street
> New York, NY 10011

*Academy of Senior Professionals:* This senior learning center is part of Eckerd College in St. Petersburg, Florida. It is different from others in two major ways: First, it is aimed at people who have distinguished themselves in a wide range of disciplines. Among its 146 participants are a Pulitzer Prize-winning novelist, a former U.S. Senator, a former ambassador to the Soviet Union, a noted historian, a British journalist, and the retired executive director of the American Institute of Banking. While everyone has not achieved the level of acclaim reflected by these few, members must bring an expertise and demonstrated achievement to the program.

The other way it differs from other senior learning centers is that it stresses intergenerational learning. About half of the Academy's members pass along their knowledge, acquired through a lifetime of success, to Eckerd College's undergraduate students and high school students in the St. Petersburg/Tampa area. Academy members also serve as career advisors and discussion leaders.

In addition to involvement with younger students, Academy members participate in classes at Eckerd College or discussion groups conducted by their peers.

The Academy does not accept all who apply. Applicants are screened by a membership committee and voted on by the Academy's thirteen-member Senate. Two criteria are used in selecting members: whether the applicants can contribute to the intellectual development of the other members, and whether they can gain fulfillment from what the Academy offers. Those selected pay a $1,000 initiation fee and $600 annual membership fee.

Members may use the Academy's library, meeting rooms, computers and dining facilities. In addition, they take boating trips on the Gulf of Mexico and join Eckerd College students at parties and luncheons. The Academy offers a rich mixture of learning, recreation and social interaction.

> Academy of Senior Professionals
> Eckerd College
> 4200 54th Avenue South
> St. Petersburg, FL 33711

*Center for Creative Retirement:* The Center for Creative Retirement is on the campus of the University of North Carolina in Asheville. It is a national model of how retirees and their communities can mutually benefit each other. The center offers a variety of programs in community leadership, retirement planning, peer teaching and learning, health promotion, and intergenerational education. It operates a research institute to study retirement issues. Activities of the Center fall under five headings:

- *Senior Leadership Seminars:* Classes prepare retirees for meaningful volunteer or entrepreneurial positions in the community.

- *The Retirement Wellnes Center:* A sixteen-hour wellness course teaches diet, stress management, exercise and positive attitudes to promote a healthy lifestyle. Graduates serve as public speakers, program planners and mentors.

- *The College for Seniors:* A peer-learning program, retirees study liberal arts courses taught by both university faculty and retirees. Courses cover art, history, literature and world affairs.

- *Retirement Issues Forums:* In a series of public forums, experts from academia, business, government and civic organizations explore issues related to aging that most affect retirees.

- *The Senior Academy for Intergenerational Learning:* The knowledge and expertise of retired professionals are utilized while they serve as mentors, tutors and counselors to the university's undergraduates.

Anyone 55 years or older is welcome at the Center. No prerequisite education or experience is required. A modest membership fee is charged with financial assistance available for eligible participants.

> Center for Creative Retirement
> University of North Carolina
> Ashville, NC 28804

**The New England Senior Academy:** This weekend residential program is on the campus of the University of New Hampshire. It is sponsored by the New England Center and the New England Land Grant Universities. Sessions begin on Friday evening with a buffet dinner and end on Sunday with brunch. Time is spent in discussions, lectures, demonstrations and special events. Each weekend focuses on a specific subject from art and literature to history and culture. Courses and discussions are led by university faculty.

> New England Senior Academy
> University of New Hampshire
> 15 Stafford Street
> Durham, NH 03824

## CONCLUSION

Whether you want to go to college for an advanced degree or take a short course on auto mechanics, there is a wealth of learning opportunities to choose from. You do not even have to leave home. Home study courses by television and correspondence are available. Your neighborhood community college and high school probably offer continuing education courses, as do the YMCA, Senior Center and churches.

Many colleges and universities, looking to capitalize on the contributions of older adults, offer special programs. In some cases, fees are eliminated or discounted. On a space available basis, arrangements can often be made for seniors to audit classes. Many programs aimed at older adults include an opportunity to volunteer your knowledge and experience, to instruct peers and serve as counselor, mentor or adviser to undergraduates. These are excellent programs to combine learning and volunteer service.

Learning opportunities can be combined with travel by taking advantage of the array of programs offered by Elderhostel, Interhostel, and other organizations. You have a choice of domestic or foreign travel and can select from a wide array of subjects. Programs including foreign travel are worthwhile alternates to typical foreign travel tours. If you plan to travel abroad, a language course in a foreign country would be an excellent way to begin your travels.

If you prefer to stay closer to home, consider taking advantage of noncredit classes offered by high schools, community colleges, and college continuing education departments. Courses cover technical skills, hobbies, general interest and high school equivalency. The public library, newspaper and the schools themselves will give you information on what is available.

To continue enjoying retirement and growing older, you must keep your mind active. There are several ways to do that. Involvement in educational activities is one of them. You are never too old to learn.

# Chapter *11* _____

# *Athletic Activities*

---

This weekend, at the TAC-USA National Masters Track and Field Championships, Anne Clarke, age 81, will run 24 times around the track while competing in the 10,000 meter run on Saturday. Thursday she won the 5,000 meter run for her age group with a time of 31:40 and Friday morning she won the 5,000 meter walk for her age group in a time of 39:03.

Clarke's interest in running began after she retired from teaching. She entered her first 10,000 meter run at age 69 and celebrated her 75th birthday by running a marathon in Paris.

*Chicago Heights Star*, July 6, 1991

---

Many activities can help keep you fit and, at the same time, add pleasure to your life. They can also bring you in contact with others who share the same interests.

Your community probably offers many kinds of sports and athletic activities. It is not necessary to join a private health club or country club to find facilities for golf, tennis or swimming. Parks and recreational departments operate tennis courts, golf courses, bicycle trails, swimming pools and skating rinks. YMCAs offer facilities for fitness and weight training, as well as for sports activities. Public bowling alleys can get you in touch with a league. Senior centers offer fitness programs such as softball games and walking groups.

If you were only an occasional participant while working, or if you are contemplating a new activity, professional lessons can get you off to a good start. It is a lot more fun when you know how to participate properly in an activity. Follow these four rules as you participate in any athletic activity:

- Be aware of your family history. Heart disease has strong genetic links.

- Before starting a fitness program, have a physical exam. High-intensity athletes should have periodic stress tests.

- Listen to your body. Warning signs such as chest pains, dizziness or numbness, especially during workouts, can signal heart disease.

- Keep your cholesterol level low and follow a low-fat diet.

---

**Potential Athletic Activities**

1. What athletic activities have you enjoyed in the past but have not participated in recently?

_____

_____

2. What athletic activities do you presently enjoy and plan to continue?

_____

_____

3. What new athletic activities would you like to try in retirement?

_____

_____

---

## SOME POPULAR ACTIVITIES

The older population actively engages in a wide range of athletic activities. Activities in this chapter represent the variety available for your consideration.

## Walking/Hiking

Walking is the most popular exercise among older people. It is considered one of the best overall exercises. It improves circulation, strengthens leg muscles, and provides a good cardiovascular workout without a lot of wear and tear on the body. The benefits of walking can be increased by adding speed and/or distance and by walking up and down hills.

Walking activities vary from regular walks in your neighborhood to walking races, walking tours, and hiking in the back woods. Whether or not your plans include walking the Appalachian Trail, by walking you can find spiritual renewal, reduced stress, physical conditioning, and an appreciation of the out-of-doors. If you are interested in moving beyond your neighborhood, these organizations have information for you:

- American Hiking Society
  1015 13th Street NW
  Washington, DC 20007

- Race Walking Committee
  Athletics Congress of the USA
  36 Canterbury Lane
  Mystic, CT 06355

  ***Publications:*** There are a number of guides to help you find your way. New editions in the Walk Series by Henry Holt include *Barcelona Walks, Beijing Walks, Jerusalem Walks,* and *New York Walks.* They are priced at $10.95 to $15.95 and are available at your local bookstore. Two new *Step-by-Step* guides by Christopher Turner feature Barcelona and Paris. They are offered by St. Martin's Press at $9.95.

## Golf

Most retirement communities include at least one golf course. Private golf and country clubs exist in nearly every community. Most communities have public courses available. With the wide availability of facilities, it is not suprising that golf is so popular with both men and women of retirement age.

Golf is a social game of skill. It serves as the catalyst for establishing, building and maintaining relationships with people who share a common interest. People with a wide range of skill enjoy golf. There is the challenge of competing against their own prior record, as well as against others of similar capabilities.

Most municipal and some private golf courses give golfers over the age of 65 a discount off of regular green fees. In highly populated areas, discounts may be restricted to certain weekdays. For avid golfers who like to travel, you cannot beat The Golf Card. Membership runs $120 for a couple the first year, and $105 thereafter. Membership entitles you to play two complimentary 18-hole rounds at about 1,700 golf courses throughout the world. You also get discounts at many resorts and a bimonthly magazine, *Golf Traveler*, which contains a directory and guide to participating courses and resorts.

> The Golf Card
> P.O. Box 6439
> Salt Lake City, UT 81406

## Tennis

An estimated four million of the nation's tennis players are over age 50. Tennis is an ideal lifetime sport that gets you out and involved with others. It improves strength, endurance and energy, helps control weight and makes you feel good. Most communities have public tennis courts; private clubs are available for those who prefer to spend less time waiting for a court.

The United States Tennis Association recognizes the value and potential of senior players, and encourages senior tennis as a healthful recreation. The Association supports recreational players through both doubles and singles leagues. It publishes a national directory of senior tennis programs, including names of contact people and the name, address and telephone number of the organizations. Membership costs $20 a year.

> United States Tennis Association
> 707 Alexander Road
> Princeton, NJ 08540

The Super-Senior Tennis group is made up of men, 55 years and older, who compete in United States Tennis Association tournaments, promote tennis for older men, and arrange tennis off-season events. For

$12 a year (tax-deductible), you receive a membership card and a bimonthly newsletter, showing tournament dates and results.

Super-Senior Tennis
P. O. Box 5165
Charlottesville, VA 22905

## Swimming

Swimming is called the perfect sport. It exercises all major muscle groups, provides a cardiovascular workout with little chance of injury, and builds endurance, strength and flexibility. According to the President's Council on Physical Fitness, swimming, with 66.1 million participants, is the most widely enjoyed of all sports.

If you join a team, a swim club, or enter competitions, swimming can also be a social activity. YMCAs and community centers offer a wide range of swimming activities, including water exercise and sports. If you do not know how to swim, or are a bit rusty, a Red Cross swim class offers an easy way to learn, in a comfortable, safe environment.

United States Masters Swimming provides opportunities to participate in organized swim activities, up to international competitions. More than 25,000 members participate in 450 local clubs. Membership includes insurance, a newsletter and a magazine with information on where to swim, groups to swim with, and tips on technique. If you enjoy competition, you can participate in local, regional, national and international meets. Competitors are placed in five-year age groups, up to 90-plus.

United States Masters Swimming
2 Peter Avenue
Rutland, MA 01543

## Bicycling

Bicycling is a popular sport with people over the age of 50. Not only is it an excellent way to stay fit, it is a useful form of transportation and a wonderful way to travel.

Bicycle touring is a great way to see the country. You travel on quiet, scenic routes through small towns and villages while enjoying nature and the out-of-doors. Many organizations run group tours all over the world for older cyclists. You do not have to be a trained athlete to enjoy a tour. The following organizations can help you get more involved with cycling:

*Bikecentennial:* This cross-country bicycle route was established in 1973, in observance of the U.S. Bicentennial. The TransAmerica Bicycle Trail is the backbone of its 17,000 mile network. Today, more than 20,000 members and 150 affiliated clubs are served by Bikecentennial. It has the largest collection of information available anywhere, including maps, tour guides, safety information and educational materials.

> Bikecentennial
> P.O. Box 8308
> Missoula, MT 59807

*League of American Wheelmen:* This national association of bicyclists protects cyclists' rights and promotes safe cycling. More than 500 affiliated clubs sponsor rides and rallies. Members receive *Bicycle USA* magazine. Each year, the *Cycling Calendar* lists over 500 events. *Bicycle USA Almanac* contains information on clubs, events, books, magazines, organizations and lobbyists. *Bicycle USA Tourfinder* will help plan your cycling adventures anywhere in the world.

> League of American Wheelmen
> 6707 Whitestone Road, Suite 209
> Baltimore, MD 21207

*The Tandem Club of America:* The bicycle built for two is making a comeback. It is ideal for touring, and each year it is one of the most exciting events at the world cycling championships. The club sends out a newsletter and promotes rallies. Membership is $10.

> Tandem Club of America
> 2220 Vanessa Drive
> Birmingham, AL 35242

*United States Cycling Federation:* As a part of the U.S. Olympic Committee, this organization conducts races for its members, who are between the ages of 9 and 89. The 80-member clubs promote activities for beginners and organize races for the more experienced. Members receive a monthly newsletter listing coming events.

United States Cycling Federation
1750 East Boulder Street
Colorado Springs, CO 80909

***Backroads Bicycle Touring:*** This tour operator offers Prime-Time Tours for cyclists over 50. Seniors are welcome to join any of their other tours, rated for Beginners, Energetic Beginners, Intermediates and Advanced cyclists. Tours are also arranged for singles.

Backroads Bicycle Touring
1516 5th Street
Berkeley, CA 94710

***American Youth Hostel Bike Tours:*** Despite its name, this organization offers tours for people over 50. Participants stay in hostels, which offer simple dormitory-style accommodations. They eat local food and meet people who enjoy the same things. Tours are limited to 10 cyclists. Recent tours have included Hawaii, Europe, New England and Wisconsin. Annual membership is $15 for those over 55.

American Youth Hostel
P. O. Box 37613
Washington, DC 20013

***The Cross Canada Cycle Tour Society:*** This club sponsors trips for all ages. Its local members get out twice a week for trips of 30 to 50 miles. While most members live in British Columbia, the Society welcomes cyclists from all over on their trips.

The Cross Canada Cycle Tour Society
1200 Hornby Street
Vancouver, BC
Canada V6Z 2E2

## Skiing

According to the National Ski Areas Association, there are more than 200,000 downhill skiers over the age of 55. Probably twice that many participate in cross-country skiing. Many ski areas encourage older skiers by providing discounts, special lessons and sometimes free use of facilities.

## Downhill Skiing

Downhill skiing provides a continual challenge for every level of skill. Each time you attain a goal, you begin looking for the next one to conquer. There is as much excitement in skiing the "bunny" slope for the first time as there is in successfully skiing the advanced slope. The following organizations support and encourage older skiers:

*70-Plus Ski Club:* All 4,500 members of this group are active downhill skiers in their 70s and 80s, with a few in their 90s. The Club meets at various ski areas, usually in New York or New England, for races, companionship and partying. Hunter Mountain in New York hosts the club's annual meeting each March, with ski racing for men ages 70 to 80, women ages 70 to 80, and everyone over 80. In addition to activities in the Eastern U.S., special events are scheduled in the Rockies and Swiss Alps. Lifetime memberships cost $5. Members receive a Club patch, a membership card, a newsletter and a list of ski areas throughout the U.S. where they can ski free or at a discount. For a small charge, a membership list can be ordered to help members arrange for companionship on their ski outings.

> 70-Plus Ski Club
> 104 East Side Drive
> Ballston Lake, NY 12019

*NASTAR:* NASTAR (National Standard Race) is sponsored by *Ski* magazine for recreational downhill skiers of all ages. Over 5,000 races are held all over the U.S. each year, for medals based on age, sex and skill level. Age divisions include men and women, ages 50 to 59, women ages 60 and over, men ages 60 to 69, and men ages 70 and over. Skiers may race on their own or as part of a participating club.

> NASTAR
> P. O. Box 4580
> Aspen, CO 81612

*United States Ski Association Alpine Masters:* A good competitive skier will enjoy the masters races for older skiers, sponsored throughout the U.S. by this organization. Those who do well in the U.S. competition can participate in the International Masters Cup. Skiers must join the U.S. Ski Association and get a racing license to be eligible for Masters races.

United States Ski Association
P. O. Box 100
Park City, UT 84060

## Cross-Country Skiing

Cross-country skiing is growing in popularity. It takes less time to learn, is safer, costs less, and is easier on you physically. In contrast to downhill, cross-country can be enjoyed any place where there is snow. And, it is a great sport to enjoy with grandchildren. There are resorts, trails, ranches and lodges all over the country where you can enjoy cross-country skiing. The Cross-Country Ski Areas Association will send you *Destinations*, a guide listing more than 500 cross-country ski areas, plus tips for beginners and coupons for lessons, equipment rentals and trail passes.

Cross-Country Ski Areas Association
259 Bolton Road
Winchester, NH 03470

*World Masters Cross-Country Ski Association:* Skiers must be over 30 years old to ski in the international races run each year by this organization. Competitors are grouped in five-year intervals, to 75 plus years old, separated by sex. In recent years, championships were held in Austria, Canada and Sweden.

World Masters Cross-Country Ski Association USA
P. O. Box 718
Hayward, WI 54843

## Horseback Riding

Package tours are available for people over the age of 60 who enjoy a trip on horseback. These trips, scheduled from May to September, ride at a more leisurely pace than the general ones. Recent destinations have been Argyll, Scotland, Alsace in France, the Black Forest of Germany, Lough Derg, Ireland, and Pleasant River, Maine. Companions who do not ride may travel the same route by car. Groups are small and are led by a guide.

Fit Equestrian, 60-Plus Club
2011 Alamo Pintado Road
Solvang, CA 93463

## Canoeing

Canoeing can be enjoyed in nearly all parts of the country; the Minnesota-Ontario Boundary Waters offer some of the best. Two packages are available for those over age 50. Senior lodge-to-lodge trips include six days camping out or sleeping in rustic fishing cabins, canoeing the rivers and lakes along the Canadian border during the day. Senior base camp trips stay in a permanent wilderness tent camp with a cook and guide, and fish and explore on their own schedule. Canoe instructions and practice are given before setting out on a trip.

> Canoe Country Escapes
> 194 South Franklin Street
> Denver, CO 80209

## MULTI-ACTIVITY ORGANIZATIONS

Several organizations offer athletic activities for older people. If you are looking for an athletic event to enjoy, your are sure to find it among the eight described below:

## The Senior Olympics

The U.S. National Senior Sports Classic is held every other year in a different host city. Participants must be at least 55 years old and place first, second or third in their age group at a local senior games event sanctioned by the organization. Over 500 events range from archery and badminton to cycling, swimming and track and field events. Less strenuous activities such as horseshoes, shuffleboard, softball and golf are also included. Athletes who want to start training for the next senior games should get a set of ground rules from the organization.

> U.S. National Senior Olympics
> 14323 South Outer Forty Road, Suite N-300
> Chesterfield, MO 63017

## World Senior Games

The World Senior Games are held annually in Saint George, Utah. Recent games attracted over 1,000 participants from 41 states and 3 foreign countries. Events include tennis, golf, horseshoes, cycling, road racing, basketball, softball, swimming and table tennis. For information write to:

Huntsmen Chemical's World Senior Games
1355 South Foothill Drive
Salt Lake City, UT 84108

## National Senior Sports Association

This association organizes competitive and recreational events in golf, tennis, fishing, bowling and skiing, at resorts around the world. All members are over 50 years old. The association uses group purchasing power and scheduling in the slower seasons to offer first-class packages at reasonable prices. Recent events have been held in Acapulco, Las Vegas, Myrtle Beach, Palm Springs, Hawaii, Ireland, Canada and other choice spots. Membership alternatives are $25 for a year, $65 for three years, and $150 for life. *Senior Sports News* keeps members up-to-date on scheduled outings.

National Senior Sports Association
10560 Main Street, Suite 205
Fairfax, VA 22030

## National Handicapped Sports

This organization promotes the participation of disabled people of all ages in sports and fitness activities. Its sixty chapters conduct such activities as camping, hiking, biking, horseback riding, water skiing, road racing, white-water rafting, mountain climbing and snow skiing. Members receive a newsletter to keep them up-to-date on competitions and other events.

National Handicapped Sports
1145 19th Street NW, Suite 717
Washington, DC 20036

## Outdoor Adventures for Women Over 40

This organization attracts physically fit women whose ages range from 40 to over 80. A little over half are married, and half are employed. They come from all over the country, though most are from New England. All love the out-of-doors.

Trips are led by trained guides and include instruction, lodging, food and transportation. Previous adventures have included a ten-day walking tour of England, a two-week hiking trip in Switzerland and France, cross-country skiing in Glacier National Park, a canoe trip in Vermont and rafting in Yellowstone National Park.

> Outdoor Vacations for Women Over 40
> P. O. Box 200
> Groton, MA 01450

## The Over the Hill Gang

This international club is for people over 50 years old who are engaged in all kinds of athletic activities. The club has 2,500 members and 15 Gangs, or chapters. Each Gang decides its own activities, which have included skiing, scuba diving, hiking, camping, fishing, hot air ballooning, surfing, canoeing and travel. If there is no chapter near you, you can become a member-at-large. Annual at-large memberships are $25 for singles and $40 for couples. Gang membership is double that. Members receive a bimonthly newsletter and discounts.

> Over the Hill Gang International
> 13791 East Rice Place
> Aurora, CO 80015

## Fit Over Fifty

Run by the Institute for Success Over Sixty, Fit Over Fifty Seminars are action programs held in Aspen, Colorado and Alta, Utah. Six-day summer seminars include hiking and rafting, along with sessions on health and nutrition, personal development, physical fitness and relationships. Along with the educational sessions, winter seminars offer instruction and performance analysis in downhill and cross-country skiing. Packages include lodging, meals and parties.

Fit Over Fifty Seminars
P. O. Box 160
Aspen, CO 81612

## Mt. Robson Adventure Holidays

This tour operator caters exclusively to the over-50 crowd. Special trips take place high in the Canadian Rockies several times each summer. Golden Week includes two days of hiking, two days of canoeing, and one day of historical touring. You sleep in heated log cabins at the base camp. Or, you can fly by helicopter to a base camp for five days of tent camping and hiking.

Mt. Robson Adventure Holidays
P. O. Box 146
Valemount, British Columbia
Canada VOE 2ZO

***American Volkssport Association (AVA):*** This association is the US affiliate of the International Volkssport Verband (IVV), formed in Germany in 1968, to organize noncompetitive activities for all ages and abilities. Sanctioned activities include walking, swimming, bicycling, skiing and roller-skating, without the hassle of vying for titles or timed finishes. Today, thirty countries are affiliated with the IVV; all 50 states have AVA chapters.

An IVV logbook for keeping an official record of events and distances costs $4.00. Patches, pins and certificates are given out at no cost after the first ten events, the next 20, the 50th, and every 25 thereafter. Patches, pins and certificates are also given for every 500 kilometers completed. Entry fees of around $5.00 per event cover the costs of awards designed to honor the event.

Volkssport news and calendars of events are published in the AVA newspaper, *The American Wanderer*, published every other month; subscriptions are $12.00 annually. State associations also publish monthly newsletters. For information on events and chapters near you, write to:

American Volkssport Association
Phoenix Square, Suite 203
1001 Pat Booker Road
Universal City, TX 78148

## CONCLUSION

Some athletic activity is appropriate for everyone, to counteract the effects of aging. Thirty percent of muscle mass is lost between the ages of 30 and 70 unless some physical activity replaces it; strength, stamina, and flexibility exercises can keep your body functioning properly into your 80s and 90s. If you neglect your body, it will atrophy. Joints will lose movement, tendons will tighten up, you will gain weight. You will become short of breath after the most modest forms of exertion.

For many people, athletic activities are more than a way to keep their bodies functioning. The activities they choose to engage in become a route to adventure, challenge and personal achievement. Physical fitness is a prerequisite to engaging in their chosen activities, such as mountain climbing, skiing, cycling, swimming, track and field events, and scuba diving.

Enthusiasts can engage in competitions and group outings where they can meet and become friends with others who share their interest, whether they are cycling through Europe, hiking in Switzerland, canoeing in Minnesota, or riding horseback in Ireland.

It is never too late to take up an interest in some form of athletic activity. Do not let age hold you back. Each month, in the newspapers, there are many examples of people taking up activities such as golf, tennis, skiing, scuba diving, cycling and hiking, after they have reached or passed 60 years old. The effects on your body will amaze you. Men and women in their 60s and 70s become as fit and energetic as the average 40 year old. Those who improve the most are most out of shape to begin with.

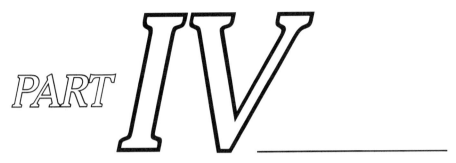

PART *IV*

# Planning
# Your
# Future

_____

# Chapter 12

# *What Do You Want to Do with Your Retirement?*

Now it is time to pull all your thoughts together and develop your plan for retirement. How will you capitalize on this "Window of Opportunity" that is opening to you? With career and family responsibilities behind you, how will you use your time to bring fulfillment? You will have written answers to these questions when you complete this chapter.

By completing the exercises in prior chapters, you have already gained some insight into what lies ahead. As you complete these exercises, examine your responses to them. Either bring your responses forward, or modify them as a result of the knowledge gained from your reading.

_____

## ASSESSMENT

To develop valid plans, you need to know what you have to work with. The assessment exercises will help you clarify information about yourself. You will first look at activities you like and dislike and draw conclusions about your skills and interests. Then you will look at your inclination to take risks. Your tolerance to take risks is an important issue to consider as you enter retirement. You may need to moderate your risk-taking, or open up more to risk, to fully experience all that retirement offers.

## Skills and Interests Assessment

To make retirement the exciting experience it can be, you need to examine your skills and interests. These attributes become the means by which you can achieve your potential.

One way to assess your skills and interests is to make a list of things you do well. Do not limit yourself to skills and interests you have demonstrated at work; skills can also be acquired at home and doing volunteer service.

There are three basic skill categories—dealing with data, dealing with people, and dealing with things.

- *Data skills* involve working with information, usually in written form—researching, comparing, computing, compiling, analyzing, organizing, copying and synthesizing.

- *People skills* involve interacting with others—negotiating, persuading, counseling, teaching, supervising, motivating, serving, helping, coordinating and organizing.

- *Things skills* involve working with tangible objects—operating, manipulating, controlling, handling, building and organizing.

*Step 1:* List the activities which describe your past and present work, volunteer, hobby and leisure pursuits. Use short sentences and action verbs to describe each activity. In the *Skills* column, identify the skill involved: use a one- or two-word phrase such as writing, selling, creating, analyzing, teaching, public speaking, building and quilting. Place a check mark in one of the next three columns, to identify the skill as a *Data, People* or *Things* skill. Place a check mark in the remaining two columns to indicate whether you liked or disliked the activity.

| Skills and Interests Assessment | | Data | People | Things | Liked | Disliked |
|---|---|---|---|---|---|---|
| Activity | Skill | | | | | |
| | | | | | | |
| | | | | | | |
| | | | | | | |
| | | | | | | |
| | | | | | | |
| | | | | | | |
| | | | | | | |
| | | | | | | |
| | | | | | | |
| | | | | | | |
| | | | | | | |
| | | | | | | |
| | | | | | | |
| | | | | | | |
| | | | | | | |
| | | | | | | |

*Step 2:* Summarize the skills demonstrated in activities you liked, within each of the three categories of *Data, People* and *Things* skills. Work from the information on your Activities List. Do the same for activities you disliked.

| Skills Summary | |
|---|---|
| Liked | Disliked |
| **Data Skills** | |
| **People Skills** | |
| **Things Skills** | |

*Step 3:* Summarize your findings by writing three paragraphs about what you have learned. First, put down your thoughts about what you like to do—the skills involved and whether you enjoy working with data, people or things. Second, comment on things you dislike doing—the skills required and whether they involve data, people or things. Third, draw some conclusions about what this means for you in retirement.

Things I like to do:

Things I dislike doing:

Conclusion:

## Risk Assessment

Risk-taking is central to the enrichment of life. Those who reach their goals often have to go out on a limb. This allows them a wider range of opportunities and fulfillment. Through risk-taking, you develop greater self-confidence, which in turn gives you a competitive edge. Of course, successful risk-taking requires some moderation. It does not mean making foolish choices. Successful risk-taking invariably breeds confidence and encourages more risk-taking. This, in turn, breeds more success and a sense of control over your destiny.

Risk-taking is involved in four aspects of life. Looking at them separately adds persepctive to the role of risk-taking in retirement:

- Your investment choices demonstrate *financial risk*. In retirement, limit financial risk to the minimum necessary to fund your living requirements. Retirees often take greater risk than necessary when they lack financial knowledge and expertise. If this is your situation, rely on a trusted financial advisor who understands your needs and goals.

- Activities you choose demonstrate *physical risks*. Mountain climbing, auto racing and sky-diving are examples of high risk physical activities. As you choose retirement activities, be aware of your level of physical conditioning and limitations. Choose activities that offer minimal physical risk.

- Your willingness to meet new people and to be open and honest with family and friends demonstrate *interpersonal risks*. Your risk is that if others really know you, they may not like you. This could lead to rejection and embarrassment. This element of risk is worth pushing. Most often, as you become more outgoing, open and honest in interpersonal relations, you develop closer and more satisfying friendships.

- *Risk of failure* often holds people back from trying new experiences. Self-imposed inhibition prevents them from enjoying the thrill of accomplishment that comes with overcoming a challenge. Retirement gives you the freedom to try and fail. It no longer goes down as a black mark on your career record. Do not retire *from life*. Take a risk and try some new adventures.

*Step 1:* Take the following quiz to learn whether, and to what extent, you take risks. Frank answers will give you the most reliable feedback.

| Risk-Taking Quiz | Often | Sometimes | Rarely | Never |
|---|---|---|---|---|
| 1. I am concerned about the impression I make and how people react to me. | | | | |
| 2. I like to stick my neck out, even if it is not warranted. | | | | |
| 3. I tend to avoid activities or situations that are a little frightening. | | | | |
| 4. I am concerned about the possibility that others may regard me as somewhat odd or strange. | | | | |
| 5. When I try something new, I become uptight or nervous. | | | | |
| 6. I enjoy doing daring, outlandish things, just for kicks. | | | | |
| 7. The thought of speaking before a group makes me anxious. | | | | |
| 8. I tend to avoid situations in which I might feel inferior. | | | | |
| 9. I tend to worry that I will say or do something wrong. | | | | |
| 10. I feel comfortable talking to strangers. | | | | |

This quiz was developed by Eugene Raudsepp, president of Princeton Creative Research, Inc., Princeton, NJ. Used by permission.

| Risk-Taking Quiz (continued) | Agree | Disagree |
|---|---|---|
| 11. I like to have my life arranged so that it runs smoothly and predictably. | | |
| 12. The one thing I dread most is to fail. | | |
| 13. I feel that life is a struggle and I have to remain vigilant to survive. | | |
| 14. I like a job that offers challenge, change and variety, even if it involves some danger and risk. | | |
| 15. I sometimes voice opinions that seem to turn some people off. | | |
| 16. I would never worry about appearing to be over my head in what I am doing. | | |
| 17. If I was offered a great new job, for which I have little of no qualifications or experience, I would accept it. | | |
| 18. I enjoy acting on a hunch, just to see what will happen. | | |
| 19. I would like to try parachute-jumping. | | |
| 20. A person cannot be too careful these days. | | |
| 21. I do not enjoy tackling a job that might involve many unknown difficulties. | | |

*Step 2:* Score your results by checking the box with your response to each item on the quiz. Record your score for each item in the column on the right. Add up your total score.

| | Often | Sometimes | Rarely | Never | Score |
|---|---|---|---|---|---|
| 1. | 1 | 2 | 3 | 4 | |
| 2. | 5 | 4 | 2 | 0 | |
| 3. | 0 | 2 | 3 | 4 | |
| 4. | 1 | 2 | 3 | 4 | |
| 5. | 1 | 2 | 3 | 4 | |
| 6. | 5 | 3 | 1 | 0 | |
| 7. | 1 | 2 | 3 | 4 | |
| 8. | 1 | 2 | 3 | 4 | |
| 9. | 1 | 2 | 3 | 4 | |
| 10. | 4 | 3 | 2 | 1 | |
| | **Agree** | **Disagree** | | | |
| 11. | 1 | 4 | | | |
| 12. | 0 | 4 | | | |
| 13. | 1 | 4 | | | |
| 14. | 5 | 0 | | | |
| 15. | 4 | 1 | | | |
| 16. | 5 | 1 | | | |
| 17. | 5 | 1 | | | |
| 18. | 4 | 1 | | | |
| 19. | 5 | 1 | | | |
| 20. | 1 | 4 | | | |
| 21. | 2 | 4 | | | |
| | TOTAL SCORE | | | | |

*Step 3:* Interpret your score by reading the comments that apply to your Total Score points:

- *65 to 90 Points*

  If you scored in this range, you tend to feed upon risk-taking and often seek out situations that others try to avoid. Your desire for stimulation leads you to engage in activities that are fast-paced, exciting, and involve considerable risk. A sense of daring gives you exhilaration.

  High scorers in this range are bold super risk-takers, inclined to indulge in many risky adventures. Living on the brink of danger provides them with a special kind of psychic ecstasy.

  Super risk-takers frequently tend to act first, impulsively, and think later. Many of them discover their rash decisions and actions result in much regret. They are easily susceptible to boredom and get very restless in routine situations.

  In retirement, those scoring in this range should moderate their risk-taking in financial matters and seek satisfaction of their adventuresome desires through non-financial endeavors.

- *33 to 64 Points*

  A score in this range indicates that you enjoy the not-so-ordinary in your life and work. You choose activities that make you feel exhilarated and energized. Risks provide you with stimulus and positive stress you would not have otherwise. Risk-taking has been the driving force behind many of your major accomplishments.

  Individuals in this middle range have a mixture of desire for excitement in some things, and for tranquility in others. They like to balance challenge with risks, to ensure that things stay on an even keel. They prefer to thoroughly investigate situations involving risk or danger. Most of the time they can cope with the risks they take. Even when they find themselves in a dangerous spot, they are able to get out of it resourcefully.

  With important matters, they tend to march to their own beat, make their own decisions, and take the consequences for their own actions. They are rarely swayed by the advice or counsel of others.

In retirement, those scoring in this range should continue to enjoy their zest for life, while they learn to appreciate the advice and counsel of experts selected to help them plan their retirement.

- *Less than 33 Points*

If you scored in this range, you are reserved and cautious, and prefer to lead a rather quiet and sheltered life. You are probably more comfortable being able to predict your daily routines than having a life full of unexpected surprises. Wherever possible, you are likely to avoid risk and instead seek security and safety.

Many people who play it safe are unhappy captives of their fears of rejection, failure and loss of face. When faced with something challenging or new, catastrophic expectations immediately pop into their heads and the voices of gloom begin their dismal prophecies— "I'll never be able to do that." "I'll be getting in over my head." "That's just too difficult for me." "The risks are too great."—giving them an excuse not to try, not to do, not to care, not to count on, and not to want things. As a result, they miss out on much that could enrich their lives.

People in this category spend considerable energy worrying about being incompetent, regardless of the situation. They tend to exaggerate the importance of most situations. They need to learn to become less inhibited and uptight, to rid their minds of doubts, and to tough out their fears. They need to give themselves permission to overestimate themselves and downplay the potential risks involved.

Unless you are able to open up to a moderate amount of risk, you will miss what retirement has to offer. Plan some activities, meet some new people, visit some new places. While some risk is necessary, avoid the temptation to swing to the extreme, especially in financial matters.

*Step 4:* Summarize your findings by writing down what you have learned about your attitude toward risk-taking. Supplement the information given for your score range with actual experiences. Then, draw some conclusions about what this means for you in retirement.

**My thoughts on risk-taking in my life:**

**How I see risk-taking in retirement:**

1. Financial Risk:

_____

_____

_____

2. Physical Risk:

_____

_____

_____

_____

3. Interpersonal Risk:

_____

_____

_____

_____

_____

4. Risk of Failure:

_____

_____

_____

_____

## Identifying Your Dreams

Nearly everyone has dreams. With retirement, you are free—within certain limits—to pursue those dreams. Think back to your teenage years. What did you dream about doing that you could not afford? As a young adult and on into middle life, was there something you wanted to do, but never had time to accomplish? In retirement, you have the time and money, so why not go for it?

A simple four step process can make your dreams come true. Many people lack the discipline to complete all four steps:

- *Dream:* Certainly, the starting point is to have a dream. Open yourself up to the possibilities of what *could be*. Do not be held back by the fear of failure.

- *Study:* Having identified a dream, study all the aspects of that course of action. What is required to accomplish it? What different pathways would lead you to the desired outcome?

- *Plan:* Now, select a plausible pathway to your dream from the knowledge you have acquired. Develop a step-by-step action plan to move from where you are now to where you would like to be. Add both time and cost estimates to each step of your plan.

- *Act:* In the final step, take action. Nothing gets done until you take the first step. Develop the discipline and commitment to your dream that will motivate you to do the work necessary to achieve it.

**What Are Your Dreams?**

1. What did you enjoy in your childhood or teenage years that you would like to do again?

 

 

 

2. What did you develop an interest in during earlier years but were unable to pursue due to lack of money or time?

 

 

 

3. Nearly everyone has said, "One of these days I am going to _____." How would you complete this sentence?

 

 

 

4. What one or two things do you want to be sure you do before you leave this world?

 

 

 

## Family Relationships Assessment

Career demands often cause people to neglect family relationships. Retirement brings an opportunity to mend fences and develop closer relationships. Depending upon the circumstances, it may take considerable work and time to move a relationship to where you would like it to be. If some of your family relationships need attention, the following ideas will be helpful:

- Initiate contact and conversation. Do not wait for the other person to come to you.

- Be willing to apologize for your prior lack of attention or whatever your situation involved.

- Demonstrate acceptance by showing a genuine interest—listening, accepting ideas, sharing ideas and being available and responsive.

- Show support for the other person's interests, goals and aspirations by not judging or evaluating.

- Work at developing trust in the relationship by not criticizing, being open and honest with your own ideas, feelings, hopes and dreams.

**Assessing Family Relations**

*Instructions:* Write a brief assessment of your relationship with each of the following family members. Note where work toward improvement may be required.

1. Parents:

_____

_____

_____

2. Spouse:

_____

_____

_____

3. Children:

_____

_____

_____

4. Grandchildren:

_____

_____

_____

5. Siblings:

_____

_____

_____

6. Other family members:

_____

_____

_____

## PLANNING

Planning is essential to achievement. It clarifies the steps necessary to reach your goal. It establishes an order and time requirement for carrying out those steps. The very act of writing down your plans will heighten your commitment to follow through and experience the satisfaction of reaching your goal.

## General

1. I plan to retire on: _____
   (Review the information you developed in Chapter 4.)

2. A perfect retirement for me will include: (Review the exercises in Chapter 4, where you wrote out your life goals and identified your retirement concerns.)

   _____

   _____

   _____

   _____

   _____

   _____

   _____

   _____

   _____

   _____

   _____

   _____

_____

_____

_____

_____

_____

_____

_____

_____

_____

_____

_____

_____

## Detailed Plans

A fulfilling retirement will include many of the elements covered in this book, plus your specific health and financial circumstances. All of these issues are probably included in your vision of a perfect retirement. In the following sections, develop a goal and action plan for each of the major facets of your life in retirement. Consider the insight you gained in the assessment exercises you completed earlier in this chapter. Before you begin, it will be helpful to look over the categories. Be sure your goal statements are specific. For example, do not say, "My goal is to be financially secure in retirement." Instead, say, "My goal is to have $2,500 a month in income, in today's dollars."

## 1. Pursuing Your Dream

Goal: _____

_____

| **Action Steps** | **Target Date** |
|---|---|
| _____ | _____ |
| _____ | _____ |
| _____ | _____ |

## 2. Family Relationships

Goal: _____

_____

| **Action Steps** | **Target Date** |
|---|---|
| _____ | _____ |
| _____ | _____ |
| _____ | _____ |

## 3. Finances

Goal: _____

_____

| **Action Steps** | **Target Date** |
|---|---|
| _____ | _____ |
| _____ | _____ |
| _____ | _____ |

## 4. Health

Goal: _____

_____

| **Action Steps** | **Target Date** |
|---|---|
| _____ | _____ |
| _____ | _____ |
| _____ | _____ |

## 5. Housing

Goal: _____

_____

| **Action Steps** | **Target Date** |
|---|---|
| _____ | _____ |
| _____ | _____ |
| _____ | _____ |

## 6. Income Producing Activities

Goal: _____

_____

| **Action Steps** | **Target Date** |
|---|---|
| _____ | _____ |
| _____ | _____ |
| _____ | _____ |

## 7. Volunteer Activities

Goal: _____

_____

| Action Steps | Target Date |
|---|---|
| _____ | _____ |
| _____ | _____ |
| _____ | _____ |

## 8. Leisure Activities

Goal: _____

_____

| Action Steps | Target Date |
|---|---|
| _____ | _____ |
| _____ | _____ |
| _____ | _____ |

## 9. Hobbies

Goal: _____

_____

| Action Steps | Target Date |
|---|---|
| _____ | _____ |
| _____ | _____ |
| _____ | _____ |

## 10. Educational Activities

Goal: _____

_____

| Action Steps | Target Date |
|---|---|
| _____ | _____ |
| _____ | _____ |
| _____ | _____ |

## 11. Athletic Activities

Goal: _____

_____

| Action Steps | Target Date |
|---|---|
| _____ | _____ |
| _____ | _____ |
| _____ | _____ |

## 12. Other

Goal: _____

_____

| Action Steps | Target Date |
|---|---|
| _____ | _____ |
| _____ | _____ |
| _____ | _____ |

## Summary

Look over the work you have done and summarize your plans. Begin by summarizing your action steps, so it will be easier for you to monitor your progress. Then, summarize your planned activities into activities you will do with your spouse (if married) and without your spouse. Schedule a follow-up review during the next year.

| 1. Summary of Action Steps | |
| --- | --- |
| **Action Steps** | **Target Date** |
| _____ | _____ |
| _____ | _____ |
| _____ | _____ |
| _____ | _____ |
| _____ | _____ |
| _____ | _____ |
| _____ | _____ |
| _____ | _____ |
| _____ | _____ |
| _____ | _____ |
| _____ | _____ |
| _____ | _____ |
| _____ | _____ |

## 2. Summary of Activities With and Without Spouse

Activities planned with spouse:

_____

_____

_____

_____

_____

_____

Activities planned without spouse:

_____

_____

_____

_____

_____

## 3. Follow-up Schedule

Following-up your plans creates an effective way for you to prod yourself to action. If you are married, do the review and follow-up with your spouse.

3-month review date: _____

6-month review date: _____

12-month review date: _____

## Plan Validation

Review your plans to see if you have built in the considerations necessary for a fulfilling retirement. You should be able to answer all of the following questions in the affirmative:

|  | Yes | No |
|---|---|---|
| 1. Have I planned activities that will replace needs—satisfaction I will lose when I quit working—identity, structure, social involvement and psychological? | ☐ | ☐ |
| 2. Have I built my plan around what I do well and what I enjoy doing? | ☐ | ☐ |
| 3. Have I factored in my inclination for risk-taking by moderating in areas where I am inclined to risk too much, and stretching in areas where I have played too safe? | ☐ | ☐ |
| 4. Have I planned some activities I can enjoy alone and some I can enjoy with others? | ☐ | ☐ |
| 5. (If married) Have I planned some activities that include my spouse, as well as some that do not include him or her? | ☐ | ☐ |
| 6. Have I planned some activities that are physically challenging, as well as some that are intellectually challenging? | ☐ | ☐ |
| 7. Will my living arrangements and surroundings accommodate my planned activities? | ☐ | ☐ |
| 8. Have I planned some activities I can continue to enjoy in later life, when I begin to experience physical limitations? | ☐ | ☐ |
| 9. Will my plans allow me to live the remainder of my life to its fullest? | ☐ | ☐ |
| 10. Have I planned to achieve all that is important to me in the time I have left? | ☐ | ☐ |

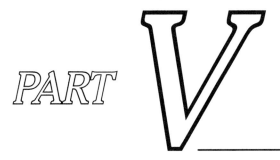

# Resource Appendix

# I. GOVERNMENT AGENCIES

Small Business Administration
1-800-827-5722

The Student Guide: Five Federal
   Programs
Federal Student Aid Program
P.O. Box 84
Washington, DC 20044

# II. CAREER PLANNING/PROFESSIONAL ASSOCIATIONS

Executive Service Corps
257 Park Avenue South
New York, NY 10010

International Executive Service
   Corps
P.O. Box 1005
Stamford, CT 06904

Howard L. Shenson
20750 Ventura Boulevard
Woodland Hills, CA 91364
1-800-703-1415

Senior Career Planning and
   Placement Service
257 Park Avenue South
New York, NY 10010

Service Corps of Retired
   Executives
1825 Park Avenue South
Washington, DC 20009

# III. VOLUNTEER REFERRAL SERVICES

AARP
Fulfillment Center
601 E Street NW
Washington, DC 20049

ACTION Volunteer Agency
   (Regional Offices)
*National Headquarters*
1100 Vermont Avenue NW
Washington, DC 20525

10 Causeway Street
Room 473
Boston, MA 02222

10 West Jackson Boulevard
6th Floor
Chicago, IL 60604

211 Main Street
Room 350
San Francisco, CA 94105

Federal Office Building
Suite 309
909 First Avenue
Seattle, WA 98174

U.S. Customs House, Room 108
2nd & Chestnut Streets
Philadelphia, PA 19106

6 World Trade Center
Room 758
New York, NY 10048

101 Marietta Street NW
Room 1003
Atlanta, GA 30323

1100 Commerce Street
Room 6 B 11
Dallas, TX 75242

Executive Tower Building
Suite 2930
1405 Curtis Street
Denver, CO 80202

American Red Cross
National Headquarters
Washington, DC 20562

National VOLUNTEER Center
1111 North 19th Street, Suite 500
Arlington, VA 22209

Robert Wood Johnson Foundation
P.O. Box 2316
Princeton, NJ 08543
1-609-452-8710

## IV. ACTIVITY CATEGORIES

### Advocacy/Service to Others

Civil Service International
Route 2, Box 506
Innis Free Village
Crozel, VA 22932

Family Friends Project
National Council on Aging
409 Third Street SW
Washington, DC 20024

Foundation for Grandparenting
P.O. Box 97
Jay, NY 12941

Habitats for Humanity
Habitat & Church Streets
Americus, GA 31709

Heifer Project International
Route 2, Box 33
Berryville, AR 72126

Legal Counsel for the Elderly
American Association of Retired
  Persons
1909 K Street NW
Washington, DC 20002

National Association of Meal
  Programs
1424 K Street NW, Suite 500
Washington, DC 20005

National CASA Association
2722 Eastlake Drive East
Seattle, WA 98102

Peace Corps
Public Response Unit
1990 K Street NW
Washington, DC 20562

Team Work
Foundation for Exceptional
  Children
1920 Association Drive
Reston, VA 22091

Volunteers in Technical Assistance
1815 North Lynn Street, Suite 200
Arlington, VA 22209

National Caucas and Center for
  Black Aged
1424 K Street NW, Suite 500
Washington, DC 20005

## Educational/Enrichment

Academy of Senior Professionals
Eckerd College
4200 54th Avenue South
St. Petersburg, FL 33711

Adult Education Association
  of the U.S.
810 18th Street NW
Washington, DC 20036

Amateur Chamber Music
  Players, Inc.
545 Eighth Avenue
New York, NY 10018

American Music Conference
303 East Wacker Drive,
Suite 1214
Chicago, IL 60601

Augusta Heritage Center
Davis and Elkins College
Elkins, WV 26241

Bagaduce Library
Green's Hill
Blue Hill, ME 04614

Betterway Publications, Inc.
Box 219
Crozert, VA 22932

Chamber Music America, Inc.
545 Eighth Avenue
New York, NY 10018

Center for Creative Retirement
University of North Carolina
Ashville, NC 28804

College-Level Examination Program
P.O. Box 6600
Princeton, NJ 08541

Council for Adult and Experiential
  Learning
226 West Jackson Street, Suite 510
Chicago, IL 60606

Country Dance and Song Society
35 East Wacker Drive, Suite 2300
Chicago, IL 60601

Department of Independent Learning
128 Mitchell Building
Pennsylvania State University
University Park, PA 16802

Foundation for Field Research
P.O. Box 2010
Watertown, MA 02272

Goddard College
Plainfield, VT 05667

The Great Books Foundation
17 New South Street
Chicago, IL 60601

Herbert Berghof Studio
120 Bank Street
New York, NY 10014

Institute for Lifetime Learning
1909 K Street NW
Washington, DC 20049

Institute for Retired Professionals
New School for Social Research
66 West 12th Street
New York, NY 10011

Library of Congress
National Library Service for the
    Blind and Physically
    Handicapped
1292 Taylor Street NW
Washington, DC 20542

Memories
Senior Software Systems
8804 Wildridge Drive
Austin, TX 78759

Music for the Love of It
67 Parkside Drive
Berkeley, CA 94705

National Home Study Council
1601 18th Street NW
Washington, DC 20009

The National Piano Foundation
4020 McEwen Street, Suite 105
Dallas, TX 75244

New England Senior Academy
University of New Hampshire
15 Stafford Street
Durham, NH 03824

Ohio University
External Student Program
309 Tupper Hall
Athens, OH 45701

Peterson's
P.O. Box 2123
Princeton, NJ 08543

Roundabout Theater Company
100 East 17th Street
New York, NY 10003

Senior Scribes
c/o Poverty Press
P.O. Box 2035
Cape May, NJ 08204

Shaw Guides
625 Baltimore Way
Coral Gables, FL 33134

The Society for the Preservation and
    Encouragement of Barbershop
    Quartet Singing in America
6315 Third Avenue
Kenosha, WI 53140

Strand Bookstore
828 Broadway
New York, NY 10003

University Research Expedition
    Programs
Desk L-02
University of California
Berkeley, CA 94720

The Writer, Inc.
120 Boylston, MA 02116

Writer's Digest
P.O. Box 2124
Harlan, IA 51593

## Environment/Horticulture

The Abundant Life Seed
  Foundation
P.O. Box 772
Port Townsend, WA 98368

The Antique Rose Emporium
Route 5, Box 143
Brenham, TX 77833

American Hiking Society Volunteer
  Vacations
P.O. Box 86
North Scituate, MA 02060

American Horticulture Society
7831 East Boulevard Drive
Alexandria, VA 22308

Brooklyn Botanic Garden
1000 Washington Avenue
Brooklyn, NY 11225

Container Gardening
Brooklyn Botanic Garden
100 Washington Avenue
Brooklyn, NY 11225

Earthwatch
P.O. Box 403N
Watertown, MA 02272

Gardener's Supply
128 Intervale Road
Burlington, VT 09401

Global Releaf
American Forestry Association
P.O. Box 2000
Washington, DC 20013

Greenpeace Action Offices

*National Headquarters*
1436 U Street NW
Washington, DC 20009

709 Center Street
Boston, MA 02130

4649 Sunnyside Avenue N
Seattle, WA 98103

Wilton Plaza, Suite 80
1881 NE 26th Street
Wilton Manors, FL 32240

1017 West Jackson Boulevard
Chicago, IL 60607

Fort Mason, Building E
San Francisco, CA 94123

Heritage Rosarium
211 Haviland Mill Road
Brookville, MD 20833

Heritage Rose Gardens
16831 Mitchell Creek Drive
Fort Bragg, CA 95437

National Audubon Society
950 Third Avenue
New York, NY 10022

National Park Service
Department of Interior
1849 C Street NW
Washington, DC 20240

Sierra Club
Public Affairs
730 Polk Street
San Francisco, CA 94104

Seed Savers Exchange
Route 3, Box 239
Decorah, IA 52101

## Hobbies/Special Interests

Accredited Genealogists
Family History Library
35 North West Temple Street
Salt Lake City, UT 84150

American Collectors Journal
P.O. Box 407
Kewanee, IL 61443

American Contract Bridge
  League
2990 Airways Boulevard
Memphis, TN 38116

American Craft Council
72 Spring Street
New York, NY 10012

American Numismatic Association
818 North Cascade Avenue
Colorado Springs, CO 80903

Anderson Arts Ranch
P.O. Box 5598
Snowmass Village, CO 81615

Ancestry Publishing
Genealogical Computing
P.O. Box 476
Salt Lake City, UT 84110

Antiques and Collecting
1006 South Michigan Avenue
Chicago, IL 60605

Arrowmont School of Arts and Crafts
P.O. Box 567
Gatlinburg, TN 37738

Association of Professional
  Genealogists
P.O. Box 11601
Salt Lake City, UT 84147

Augusta Heritage Center
Davis and Elkins College
Elkins, WV 26241

Board of Certification of
  Genealogists
P.O. Box 19165
Washington, DC 20036

Coin World
P.O. Box 150
Sidney, OH 45365

Collector Communication, Inc.
170 Fifth Avenue
New York, NY 10010

Consumer Products
American Foundation for the Blind
15 West 16th Street
New York, NY 10011

Crafting Today
P.O. Box 517
Mount Morris, IL 61054

The Crafts Fair Guide
P.O. Box 5062
Mill Valley, CA 94962

The Doll Hospital School
Lifetime Career Schools
2251 Barry Avenue
Los Angeles, CA 90064

Education Department—R
American Philatelic Society
P.O. Box 8000
State College, PA 16803

The Elder Craftsmen Shop
851 Lexington Avenue
New York, NY 10021

Family Roots
Quinsept, Inc.
P.O. Box 216
Lexington, MA 02173

Flaghouse
150 North MacQuesten Parkway
Mount Vernon, NY 10550

Genealogy Publishing Co., Inc.
1001 North Calvert Street
Baltimore, MD 21202

Genealogy Unlimited, Inc.
P.O. Box 537
Orem, UT 84059

Goodspeed's Book Shop, Inc.
7 Beacon Street
Boston, MA 02108

Haystack Mountain School of
   Crafts
Deer Isle, ME 04627

Hobby House Press, Inc.
900 Fredrick Street
Cumberland, MD 21502

Jacques Cattell Press
R.R. Bowker Company
245 West 17th Street
New York, NY 10011

Library of Congress
Washington, DC 20540

Linn's Stamp News
P.O. Box 29
Sidney, OH 45365

Modern Handcraft, Inc.
P.O. Box 5967
Kansas City, MO 64111

National Archives Records Service
General Service Administration
Washington, DC 20408

National Genealogical Society
4527 17th Street North
Arlington, VA 22207

The New York Public Library
Genealogy Division,
Room 315 N-M
Fifth Avenue and 42nd Street
New York, NY 10018

Ozarks Arts and Crafts Fair
    Association
Route 1, Box 157
Hindsville, AR 72738

Penland School
Penland, NC 28765

Puzzle Buffs International
1772 State Road
Cuyahoga Falls, OH 44223

Stamp Collector
P.O. Box 10
Albany, OR 97321

Stamps
85 Cantisteo Street
Harnell, NY 14843

Standard Doll Company
23-83 31st Street
Long Island City, NY 11105

U.S. Chess Federation
186 Route 9W
New Windsor, NY 12553

Worldwide Games
Colchester, CT 06415

United Federation of
    Doll Clubs, Inc.
P.O. Box 14152
Parkville, MO 64152

U.S. POSTAL SERVICE
Philatelic Division
Washington, DC 20265

## Travel

American Association of
    Geographers
1710 16th Street NW
Washington, DC 20009

American Association of
    Retired Persons
Special Services Department
1909 K Street NW
Washington, DC 20049

Blue Penguin Publications
147 Sylvan Avenue
Leonia, NJ 07605

Close Up Foundation
1235 Jefferson Davis Highway
Arlington, VA 22202

Cornell's Adult University
626 Thurston Avenue
Ithaca, NY 14850

Council Travel
Eurocentre Department
205 East 42nd Street
New York, NY 10017

Elderhostel
80 Boylston Street, Suite 400
Boston, MA 02116

Evergreen/Travel Club
P. O. Box 441
Dixon, IL 61021

Golden Companions
P. O. Box 754
Pullman, WA 99163

The Good Sams Club
P. O. Box 500
Agoura, CA 91303

GrandTravel
The Ticket Counter
6900 Wisconsin Avenue
Chevy Chase, MD 20815

Interhostel
University of New Hampshire
6 Garrison Avenue
Durham, NH 03824

International Friendship Service
22994 El Toro Road
El Toro, CA 92630

Loners on Wheels, Inc.
P. O. Box 1355
Poplar Bluff, MO 63901

Mature Outlook, Inc.
1500 West Shore Drive
Arlington Heights, IL 60004

Mature Traveler
P. O. Box 50820
Reno, NV 89513

The National Council of Senior
  Citizens
925 15th Street NW
Washington, DC 20005

Office of Passport Services
Bureau of Consumer Affairs
U. S. Department of State
1425 K Street NW
Washington, DC 20525

Oxford-Cambridge University
  Vacations
9602 NW 13th Street
Miami, FL 33172

Peterson's
P. O. Box 2123
Princeton, NJ 08543

Pilot Books
103 Cooper Street
Babylon, NY 11702

Saga Holidays
120 Boylston Street
Boston, MA 02116

Senior Citizen Travel Director
6633 Carlston Avenue
Oakland, CA 94610

September Days Club
751 Buford Highway NE
Atlanta, GA 30324

Shaw Guides, Inc.
625 Biltmore Way
Coral Gables, FL 33134

Travel Companion Exchange, Inc.
P. O. Box 833
Amityville, NY 11701

The Travelers' Society
P.O. Box 2846, Loop Station
Minneapolis, MN 55402

University of California Berkeley
  Extension
2223 Fulton Street
Berkeley, CA 94720

## Recreation/Sports

American Alliance for Health,
  Physical Education, Recreation,
  and Dance
1900 Association Drive
Reston, VA 22091

American Hiking Society
1015 13th Street NW
Washington, DC 20007

American Volkssport Association
Phoenix Square, Suite 203
1001 Pat Booker Road
Universal City, TX 78148

American Youth Hostel
P.O. Box 37613
Washington, DC 20013

Backroads Bicycle Touring
1516 5th Street
Berkeley, CA 94710

Bikecentennial
P.O. Box 8308
Missoula, MT 59807

Canoe Country Escapes
194 South Franklin Street
Denver, CO 80209

Country Dance and Song Society
17 New South Street
Northampton, MA 01066

The Cross Canada Cycle Tour
  Society
1200 Hornby Street
Vancouver, BC
Canada V6Z 2E2

Cross-Country Ski Areas
  Association
259 Bolton Road
Winchester, NH 03470

Dance Exchange, Inc.
1746 B Kalorama Road NW
Washington, DC 20009

Dancing USA
10600 University Avenue NW
Minneapolis, MN 55433

Fit Equestrian, 60-Plus Club
2011 Alamo Pintado Road
Solvang, CA 93463

Fit Over Fifty Seminars
P.O. Box 160
Aspen, CO 81612

The Golf Card
P.O. Box 6439
Salt Lake City, UT 81406

Huntsmen Chemical's World
  Senior Games
1355 South Foothill Drive
Salt Lake City, UT 84108

League of American Wheelmen
6707 Whitestone Road, Suite 209
Baltimore, MD 21207

Mt. Robson Adventure Holidays
P.O. Box 146
Valemount, British Columbia
Canada V0E 2Z0

National Handicapped Sports
1145 19th Street NW, Suite 717
Washington, DC 20036

National Senior Sports Association
10560 Main Street, Suite 205
Fairfax, VA 22030

National Square Dance Directory
P.O. Box 54055
Jackson, MS 39288

NASTAR
P.O. Box 4580
Aspen, CO 81612

Outdoor Vacations for Women
  Over 40
P.O. Box 200
Groton, MA 01450

Over the Hill Gang International
13791 East Rice Place
Aurora, CO 80015

Race Walking Committee
Athletics Congress of the USA
36 Canterbury Lane
Mystic, CT 06355

70-Plus Ski Club
104 East Side Drive
Ballston Lake, NY 12019

Super-Senior Tennis
P.O. Box 5165
Charlottesville, VA 22905

Tandem Club of America
2220 Vanessa Drive
Birmingham, AL 35242

United States Cycling Federation
1750 East Boulder Street
Colorado Springs, CO 80909

United States Masters Swimming
2 Peter Avenue
Rutland, MA 01543

United States Ski Association
P.O. Box 100
Park City, UT 84060

United States Tennis Association
707 Alexander Road
Princeton, NJ 08540

U. S. Amateur Ballroom Dancer
  Association
8102 Glen Gary Road
Baltimore, MD 21234

U. S. National Senior Olympics
14323 South Outer Forty Road,
  Suite N-300
Chesterfield, MO 63017

World Masters Cross-Country Ski
  Association USA
P.O. Box 718
Hayward, WI 54843

# *About the Author*

Marion Haynes retired in 1991 as Manager of Pensioner Relations for Shell Oil Company in Houston, Texas, concluding a 35-year career with Shell in Human Resources Management. Following retirement, he and his wife moved to Springdale, Arkansas.

Mr. Haynes has served on the Board of Directors of the International Society for Retirement Planning since 1988. He was elected vice president in 1989, and was installed as president in 1991. Previously, for four years he was on the Board of Directors of Sheltering Arms in Houston, a social service agency that helps the elderly maintain an independent lifestyle. At Sheltering Arms, he chaired the Personnel Committee and served on the Executive Committee.

A well-known author and public speaker, this is Mr. Haynes' seventh book. It pulls together his knowledge and experiences he has acquired working with Shell Oil Company pensioners, Houston's elderly, the International Society for Retirement Planning, and while planning and implementing his own retirement.

Mr. Haynes earned his B.S. degree in Business Administration from Arizona State University and his MBA degree, with distinction, from New York University.

# NOTES

We hope you enjoyed this book. If so, we have good news for you. This title is part of the best-selling *FIFTY-MINUTE*™ *Series* of books. All *Series* books are similar in size and identical in price. Several are supported with training videos (identified by the symbol Ⓥ next to the title).

*FIFTY-MINUTE* Books and Videos are available from your distributor. A free catalog is available upon request from Crisp Publications, Inc., 1200 Hamilton Court, Menlo Park, California 94025.

*FIFTY-MINUTE Series Books & Videos organized by general subject area.*

**Management Training:**

| | | |
|---|---|---|
| Ⓥ | Coaching & Counseling | 68-8 |
| | Conducting Training Sessions | 193-7 |
| | Delegating for Results | 008-6 |
| | Developing Instructional Design | 076-0 |
| Ⓥ | Effective Meeting Skills | 33-5 |
| Ⓥ | Empowerment | 096-5 |
| | Ethics in Business | 69-6 |
| | Goals & Goal Setting | 183-X |
| | Handling the Difficult Employee | 179-1 |
| Ⓥ | An Honest Day's Work: Motivating Employees | 39-4 |
| Ⓥ | Increasing Employee Productivity | 10-8 |
| Ⓥ | Leadership Skills for Women | 62-9 |
| | Learning to Lead | 43-4 |
| Ⓥ | Managing Disagreement Constructively | 41-6 |
| Ⓥ | Managing for Commitment | 099-X |
| | Managing the Older Work Force | 182-1 |
| Ⓥ | Managing Organizational Change | 80-7 |
| | Managing the Technical Employee | 177-5 |
| | Mentoring | 123-6 |
| Ⓥ | The New Supervisor—Revised | 120-1 |
| | Personal Performance Contracts—Revised | 12-2 |
| Ⓥ | Project Management | 75-0 |
| Ⓥ | Quality at Work: A Personal Guide to Professional Standards | 72-6 |
| | Rate Your Skills As a Manager | 101-5 |
| | Recruiting Volunteers: A Guide for Nonprofits | 141-4 |
| | Risk Taking | 076-9 |
| | Selecting & Working with Consultants | 87-4 |
| | Self-Managing Teams | 00-0 |
| | Successful Negotiation—Revised | 09-2 |
| | Systematic Problem Solving & Decision Making | 63-7 |

**Human Resources & Wellness (continued):**

**Communications & Creativity:**

**Customer Service/Sales Training:**